The Circle of Creation

Every blessing!
John Eaton.

John Eaton

The Circle of Creation

Animals in the Light of the Bible

Illustrations by Sister Theresa Margaret CHN

SCM PRESS LTD

0 334 02619 9

*Royalties from the sale of this book will be donated to the
Farm Animal Sanctuary, Post Office Cottage,
Stoney Lane, Broad Heath, Bromsgrove,
Worcs B60 1LW*

First published 1995
by SCM Press Ltd
9–17 St Albans Place London N1 0NX

Typeset at The Spartan Press Ltd, Lymington, Hants
Printed and bound in Great Britain by
Mackays of Chatham PLC, Chatham, Kent

Contents

For the animals
and those who care for them
at the Farm Animal Sanctuary

May we see that they do not live for us alone,
but for themselves and for you,
and that they love the sweetness of life.

From a prayer of St Basil for the animals

Gentle and wise in old age

Foreword

The sign of the cross invites us to connect – to connect all
that we value in life, to see in one pattern our deepest beliefs
and experiences. If I consider how I have come to write this
non-technical presentation of the Bible's view of animals, I
see it has all been about connecting. Such academic
knowledge as I have – oriental languages, biblical interpretation – had to join with the simple and profound loves of
my life to tell one story, sing one song.

Ever since SCM Press many years ago commissioned
my first book, I have wanted to write on a subject of
more instant appeal. Obadiah, Nahum, Habakkuk and
Zephaniah, the subjects of that early work, doubtless had
their importance, but it seemed to have eluded most of my
friends. How good it would be, I felt, to have the Hebrew
Bible heard on a matter near to the hearts of most people! It
was the theme of animals which gradually grew in my mind.
Even when I was writing an introduction to Hebrew,
passages like that of the donkey that spoke, or the advice to
contemplate the harvester ant, pressed themselves into the
exercises.

Against this background, two modern animals played
their part. First there was a large red tabby cat called Tiger.
Throughout his nineteen years he was a constant and
affectionate companion, comically boisterous in his youth,
gentle and wise in old age. He was in close attendance at the

production of many a work of biblical exposition. His ample and relaxed form would often fill the 'In' tray, and a painting of this scene on my wall at the university calmed the nerves of many an interviewee or new student. His deeds and qualities often prompted people to say, 'You ought to write a book about him!' His book has not yet been written, but he sowed a seed. He made me think often of the friendship of animals in the context of biblical study. There is this urge to connect all that is true.

The other animal that specially facilitated this book was one of the three hundred animals, sick or injured through callous treatment, nursed and given a home in the Farm Animal Sanctuary near Tardebigge in North Worcestershire. A national newspaper had commissioned journalist Janet Taylor to investigate conditions in animal markets and on the export trail. From the response to her revealing articles she was able to start the sanctuary, basing it as well as she could on enclosures and barns in the corner of a larger area of fields. The dream of owning a whole farm, where all the animals could be kept happily, benefitting visitors, has yet to be realized.

My wife Margaret and I had first visited the sanctuary to make a donation in memory of our late neighbour Lilian, and with several subsequent visits had got to know many of the animals and their stories, and the scale of the task Janet had undertaken. The idea of writing a biblical book on animals which might help in some way became insistent in my mind. But to *start* writing can be like getting a huge boulder to roll.

One day as we passed down the lane beside the enclosures, a white goat approached. He looked at me steadily. Perhaps he stirred a reminiscence deep in my mind of the goat for Atonement Day in ancient Israel, the goat that was singled out to bear all the sins of the people away into the wilderness. At all events, there was some sort of representation of the sufferings of many creatures, and some communication more effective than words, and I was impelled to go home and start writing at once, however inadequately.

It was not difficult to list many passages in the Bible which featured animals significantly. Many were the references to lions and lambs, ravens and reptiles, donkeys, and even dragons. There was commendation of one who 'knew the soul of his animal'. But how to bring it all together, including the first making of them, the last visions of animal forms in heaven, the stories, the proverbs, the strange practice of worshipping God through sacrifice of animals, and the vast thought of the salvation of the world through One like a sacrificial animal, the lamb slain from the foundation of the world?

As I pored over these animal elements in the Bible, a pattern began to emerge. There was the ideal of a loving community of all the species, an ideal presented, through the creation stories, as fundamental to God's eternal purpose. There was the understanding of the present world as fallen from God's ideal, but still restrained and guided in respect of animals by sacred laws. And there was the prophetic vision that the original ideal would, by God's action, at last be achieved.

But there was something else, something urgent for the present. This was the ability of the ideal world already to penetrate our fallen world with shafts of its light. Especially in the great moments of worship, there was awareness of the universal circle of praise, where all the species unite about the Creator. In these moments, knowledge fills the humble heart that here is the true and enduring world, a kingdom one can have part in *this very day*.

It seemed to me that those who now did what they could for God's abused ones, of whatever kind, were letting in the light of that true world. The oppression worldwide might seem little diminished. But the work of rescue and care was still something decisive, a crucial opening for the total victory that would appear in God's time.

I found very helpful the work of George Cansdale, *Animals of Bible Lands* (Paternoster Press 1970). This is a zoological treatment, based on first-hand experience of a great range of animals. More recently Andrew Linzey has provided an excellent and comprehensive theological discussion, *Animal Theology* (SCM Press 1994). But for myself, I felt I should keep close to the Bible's way of expression, a homely way of story, poetry and picture. I hope it will be read easily, and so bring to many a clearer notion of the place of animals in God's world and heart.

In due course my pages were enriched by the drawings of Sister Theresa Margaret CHN, and thanks to the guidance and skill of SCM Press, especially Margaret Lydamore, the work was completed. I warmly thank these colleagues, as also my wife Margaret.

John Eaton

June 1995

Foundations

The importance of animals

The botany teacher often led his young pupils through woods and by streams. One morning, when they had been considering the dragon-fly, he had told them how in many years of outdoor study he had never seen a dragon-fly lay eggs. One small boy felt sad for his teacher. And then, soon after, a little miracle happened: a dragon-fly alighted on the teacher's hand and then moved on to a near-by leaf and injected her eggs.

Many years later, the pupil remembered that moment of wonder when he heard someone read a story of Celtic times. In that story it was related that St Kevin had gone to a very lonely place to keep Lent. There he lived in a poor hut, where he would kneel to pray, his arm stretched through the window, hand open to heaven.

One day a blackbird settled on Kevin's hand and began to lay. With all gentleness and patience, Kevin cupped his hand, kept his arm steady, and was careful not to disturb her all the days till her young were hatched.

When the story was read, there was, not surprisingly, discussion about elements of exaggeration in tales of the saints. But the man who remembered the dragon-fly knew that there are moments when we can enter a world of love and trust between the species, and see miracles. He was struck by the thought that it was as Kevin knelt before God, quiet and open, that the wild creature had come to him in perfect trust. And as Kevin lived in love for God, so he was filled with love for all God's creatures.

The importance of an animal, and indeed of any creature, is that it is part of God's world, loved by him. If we respect and care for a creature, we are in harmony with God. We receive much blessing. If we despise and abuse an animal, we close ourselves off from the good world. We lose touch with God. We injure all our relationships.

As we follow the stories of animals and birds through the Bible – donkeys, ravens, lions, lambs and many others – we shall meet the ideal of a community of creatures where no harm is done. We shall meet animals that serve God, trust him, and praise him. We shall meet animals that bring us God's help, and animals that teach us of innocence and purity, loyalty and wisdom.

Intuitions of peace

The Bible has several ways of imagining the beginnings of the world. The various accounts are like poems which celebrate particular values, rooting them in the very essence of existence. Two of these accounts of the beginnings are built together in Genesis 1 – 3. Each account has its own angle on animals.

The first story (1.1 – 2.4a) imagines a beautiful order emerging from chaos. In measured stages the Creator speaks. Step by step, without haste, the orders of time and space come into being. With the succession of light and dark, the first days of the first week take their course, and on each day the Creator calls new things into being. When the seas are gathered to their places and the earth has brought forth all kinds of plants, and the lights of heaven are set to rule the orders of time, the fifth day comes – the birthday of the multitudes that are to live in the seas and skies:

And God said,
Let the waters swarm a swarm of living souls,
and winged ones wing across earth
    and the face of the arch of heaven!

From whales to little fish and birds, all in their distinctive
kinds, with their special abilities and beauties, so they are
made, in this breath-taking story, on the first of the days we
call Thursday. God looks at them all and sees that they are
good. He speaks to them, and he blesses them, making them
fertile.

Then the story brings us to the last working day of that
wonderful week, the day we call Friday. Close in time to the
creation of fish and birds, but closer still to that of humans,
comes the appearance of land animals born from the earth:

And God said,
Let the earth bring forth
living souls in due kind –
cattle and those that creep
and animals of the wild,
    all in due kind.

And all these kinds, in all their several beauties, God sees
and enjoys.

And straightaway the story comes to its other big event
for that day – the creation of the human race, male and
female. Of these it is especially said that they are created
with a divine likeness, in the very image of God. Also it is
said that they are to subdue the earth and have dominion
over all the other kinds of living souls.

Now if we were to take the story to mean that our race
was far superior and was authorized to dispose of earth and
creatures as it pleased, we would be making a fatal mistake.
True, the language is strong – to be like God, to tread down

foes, to dominate. But it is the language of ancient kingship, and in the ideals of the ancient world kingship was holy; it was God's way of maintaining goodness and care on earth. The king was promised victorious power in the strongest terms because God meant that goodness should prevail. But the king's task was above all to defend the needy and to mirror God's creative love. He was to be a good shepherd, ready to die for his flock.

So the story means to say that when all the abundance of animal souls was made, God gave them a shepherd, a supreme carer, with all the strength for the daunting task. Here was one to represent God, doing God's will on earth. Such was the human being, and such was its commission.

Our story tells of a peaceful beginning to this 'reign'. By God's command, all creatures including mankind were to feed only on the plants and fruits. Later chapters of Genesis would recognize a sad deterioration, when the many species would prey on each other (6.5–7; 9.1–7). But great prophets, looking deep into the nature of love, still knew that an age would come again when the creatures would not harm each other, but live together in trust under a king who mirrored God's goodness and power (Isa. 11.1–9; 65.25).

The account of the week of Creation ends with a day free of work. There is no rush of last-minute jobs to be done. In measured calm all has been completed when the seventh day comes. And this is the day God specially 'blesses' and 'hallows'. In blessing it he makes it fruitful; yes, rest and contemplation, a time for appreciation and fellowship, a restful time in its proper time – this is the most fruitful time of all.

In making it 'holy', he makes it a day when hearts are specially set on him, when all recollect themselves before him and are glad in his presence. It is a day to know afresh that all is his, who Only Is.

Later in the Bible the Ten Commandments will include a

4

command to keep this weekly day of recollection and communion. It is said that in this we are to follow the Creator's own example (so Ex. 20.11), and to do so also out of consideration for animals (Ex. 23.12). This teaching unfolds what has already been given in our first story: the resting of God is a time of loving relation with all the species. Animals, people and God look to each other, eye into eye, with no other concern but to be glad of each other. Animals are still good at this. You may see a trace of that far-off happy time in the eyes of a horse over a gate, or a dog by the fireside.

As I was sketching the foregoing pages, Ann came round from next door. She gave us news of her two elderly cats in brisk and cheerful tones, but we could see she was holding off a torrent of tears. She had just realized that seventeen-year-old Prudence, a dark and pretty tortoiseshell, had gone blind. This was why the cat fell when she jumped on to her favourite ledge.

Next day the vet diagnosed detached retinas but assured Ann that Prudence could still live contentedly. Ann was much relieved, having dreaded advice to put an end to her. There could be no doubt that everything would be done for Prudence that love could do.

And here also was an echo of the first golden time. The human being held sovereign power, even to kill or to keep alive, but it was a responsibility held from the Creator of all creatures, the strong serving the weak, and caring with a heart compassionate as God's.

Animals as the good companions

The inspired story of the week of creation has given us much food for thought. Study as we may, we shall never exhaust its meaning. But as if that weren't enough, we are given at once another story of the Dreaming, the time

Animals are still good at this

beyond time which is always near us; it is a child-like story and yet deeper still (Gen. 2.4a – 3.25).

Only one day is mentioned here, the day when heaven and earth were made. The Creator now has a personal name, 'Yahweh', which may mean 'He (who) is', the absolute and sovereign Reality. Our Bibles usually put for this name 'the Lord'. On this day, before any plant or animal, Man is fashioned like a clay figurine, and then animated by a puff of the Lord's breath.

The Lord then prepares a delightful garden and places the Earth-man in it to care for it. But it does not seem right for the man not to have a companion, so the Lord goes to the lengths of fashioning every kind of animal and bird and bringing them to meet the Man. As each was brought the Man gave it a name, the name it would always have. He will have looked carefully at each one, to speak to it its appropriate name. Relationship was made, and the one who gave the name became as it were the parent, bound to guide and protect.

For perfect companionship the Lord decides to go a step further. From the place of tender emotions he takes out the Man's lowest rib as he sleeps deeply, and fashions from it Woman. An inspired imagination has here given us a story to characterize the unique love of man and woman. The steps are dramatic: the ideal setting for Man – but not enough; the amazing procession of all animals – not enough; the taking and shaping of his rib, his own body's sacrifice – yes, enough now for a love truly healing and creative.

The position of the animals and birds in this sequence is significant. They are made as companions for the Man, that he should not be alone and sad. The Lord brings them to him in the beautiful orchard, one by one, and each is named and recognized as a friend. Later, Woman is made. So the origin of the human pair both precedes and follows the making of the animals, forming as it were a protective envelope around them. They are thus a central part of the story of human origins. They have a companionship to offer, and in their own way are necessary for human happiness.

In 1934 the learned scholar Helen Waddell published her translations entitled *Beasts and Saints*. From Latin documents of the Middle Ages she had selected forty-four stories of companionship between animals and hermits. We meet a monk who lived at the foot of a mountain in the burning Egyptian desert. With the help of his ox that drew up water from a deep well, he made a garden of herbs for both to live on. Of an evening he would walk some miles to a palm tree and gather dates, and there a lion would wait for him and quietly accept some dates from his hand.

We hear too of a hermit visited every evening by a wolf. She would sit outside his tiny hut, wait for a morsel from his poor meal, and lick his hand in friendship.

Another Egyptian hermit, St Macarius, once heard a knock at his door and opened it. There in the doorway stood a hyena. In her mouth she carried a cub, which he found to be blind. She had come to seek his help.

In the scrub near the River Jordan, so another story goes, Abbot Garasimus met a lion that showed him an injured paw. The monk drew out a large thorn, cleansed and bound the paw, and would have sent the lion away. But the animal would not leave him and remained his companion for many years. When the Abbot died and was buried, the lion lay upon the grave and grieved himself to death.

Helen's collection of mediaeval records includes the account of St Kevin and the blackbird which we have already considered. We hear also of St Columba of Iona and his uncanny sympathy with a crane and with a horse. We hear of St Columban in the Vosges who was surrounded and nuzzled by twelve wolves and left unharmed. This saint would walk in the woods praying, and many wild creatures would come to be stroked or to frisk about him. A squirrel would come at his call and run on his shoulder, in and out of the folds of his cowl.

And many other such stories Helen presents for us – of a sow, a wren, otters, ravens, wild geese, a cow, a hare, wild deer, sea-birds, a stag, a fox, a badger, a cock, a mouse, and even a fly that helped St Colman keep his place on the page of his holy book.

Such treasure of stories comes from people who through the love of God found a new love of animals, found it as though from the mists of the Dreaming, the far-off time which is yet so near, where the Lord fashions every creature for our friendship.

A similar thought is expressed by the seventh-century hermit Isaac of Nineveh, whose writings, long buried from sight, are being wonderfully recovered and translated by Dr Sebastian Brock in Oxford. The humble man, says Isaac, can approach wild animals. As soon as they see him, they become gentle, come to him happily and lick his hands and feet. For they scent from him the scent of Adam before the Fall, when they came to Adam to receive their names.

Animals and people in a fallen world

And that brings us to the Fall, the fateful turn in the story of the Garden of Eden (Gen. 3). Having expressed the ideal of love, the Hebrew bard has to make a link to the world we at present experience, the world of temptation, sin and estrangement. To symbolize temptation, he chooses the mysterious snake, which he calls the ablest of the animals the Lord had made. The snake, imagined as at that time able to walk like other animals, and also to talk without causing surprise, engaged the Woman in coversation about a rule which God had laid down. With his clever talk he was able to raise doubts about the Lord's guidance. The woman could not resist the prospect of gaining powerful knowledge, and the Man followed her thoughtlessly. The happy relationships were shattered. The humans took the path of power-bestowing knowledge, and learnt ever new ways of doing evil.

The inspired bard built his story from what he saw in his own day, as he looked deep into the motives and ways, ideals and betrayals of the human heart he knew. He does not have a theory about the ultimate origin of evil. So we cannot put too many questions to his snake. But we can make some points for our purpose.

Above all we read from the story that as people and animals were together in bliss, so they are together in the Fall, and together also in the bitter consequences, when fear, hate and killing prevail. And as Isaiah was to see so clearly, together they will be when the first ideal triumphs, and the baby will play with his friend the snake (Isa. 11.8).

Animals and people are certainly together in the most famous of biblical animal stories – Noah's Ark (Gen. 6 – 9). Creatures of every kind cooped up for a year with Noah's family in a boat not half the size of the Queen Elizabeth, but roofed and sealed, and battered by an all-engulfing mother of storms!

The story is built from two differing Hebrew accounts, which are themselves late forms of a story that can be traced far back to the Sumerians and their early civilization in Southern Iraq. Its main message, as we have it in Genesis, is of reassurance in a precarious world. There is frank recognition of corruption and of how the life of the whole world hangs, as it were, on a thread. There is recognition, too, of the Creator's will for righteousness and of his power of judgment. But against the terror and despair which this situation would evoke is set a compassion that will have the last word.

When we see what ruin human greed persists in causing,

when we know what catastrophe it must bring, we must learn from Noah's story that God's promise undergirds our world. Not at man's whim, but while God wills the fruitful seasons continue. He will determine the end and the outcome beyond the end, and all who now hold to the good and do what they can in tenderness for all species, will have reason to be glad. Beyond the havoc of the storm, they see the bow in the clouds and know that God keeps faith.

Solomon Raj is an Indian artist and a Lutheran pastor. He excels in expressing biblical scenes in an Indian idiom, especially in woodcuts and batiks. He works so freely from the heart, with bold shape and colour, that I tell him he is the Indian Van Gogh. On our wall is a batik he made of Noah's Ark. It is a large hand which Noah holds up to God, and large too is the dove flying back with the olive twig. The hand has worked for others and is strong in gesture of prayer and praise. The dove brings proof of the Creator's faithfulness – she is large in the artist's heart.

But for us the picture serves to show especially the unity of humans and animals. There are several decks, but one boat. All species have suffered together in the calamity. All species are represented in the rescue and the new beginning. The Ark, Solomon shows us, is a wonderful symbol of the one greater family of living souls, animals and people, intended as such by their Creator, treated as such by him, restored as such beyond the ultimate disaster.

Clean and unclean

One of the strands used in the present story of Noah's Ark states that a male and female from every species went aboard (Gen. 6.19). But the other strand tells of seven pairs of all clean creatures, and one pair of unclean (7.2). What is this 'clean' and 'unclean'? Not what we might think, for in the ancient priestly language a cow would be classed as 'clean' and a cat as 'unclean'! No, the term 'clean', *tahor*, denotes animals permitted in sacrifice and consequently also in meals. It was a matter of great concern to the priests, who drew up lists and definitions (Lev. 11; Deut. 14). But the reasons for the particular classifications are lost in the mists of time. No doubt they reflect extremely ancient tribal traditions.

What is significant is that, in the Hebrew view, when the eating of animals came to be permitted in a deteriorated world (Gen. 9.2–4), the matter was divinely regulated. The instruction after the Flood only stipulates that the animal's blood was not to be consumed (Gen. 9.4); the blood represented the living soul (*nephesh*), offered back to God in the sacrificial ritual. Later came the laws of animals permitted as food and those not permitted, the 'clean' and the 'unclean'. As long as the society had easily accessible shrines, the animals to be eaten were killed only at the shrines, with parts of the body, especially the life-blood, being symbolically offered to God.

Thus, although the highest ideal had been dimmed, the permission to kill and eat animals was not a renunciation of respect for their life and soul. The sacred laws of what was permitted, and the link with holy sacrifice, meant that reverence for all life and obedience to a higher law should still oppose the instincts of greed and cruelty.

In the New Testament the ever stricter regulation of permitted and forbidden food came to be seen as a wall that had grown high between Jew and Gentile. With a gospel for all nations, the apostles saw that this wall must come down (Acts 10). But Christians still do well to respect what underlay the old food laws. In this spirit, they must deal with their farm animals with first thought for God, not money.

Learning from animals

With people and animals regarded as a single community, with every species respected as creatures of God, it was natural for teachers to notice that people often fell below standards maintained even in a fallen world by animals. Just as we today often hear of a dog whose faithfulness puts humans to shame, so the great book of Isaiah begins with a telling contrast between the constancy of animals and the ingratitude and infidelity of the nation. Ox and ass know their owner. Working with him daily, they are attached to him and heed him, and readily return to their own stable and crib. But though the Lord has reared the Israelites as his own children, they have rebelled and sinned against him, no longer knowing where they belong, nor to whom they owe all.

Our late neighbour Lilian often recollected stories of her father's cart-horse. Her eyes would be moist and full of wonder as she recalled the animal's wise and faithful ways. Her father would set off with a cart-load of his vegetables, fruit and flowers to the Birmingham market, some fourteen miles away, and most of the miles down the city roads. Returning in the early morning, he could safely fall asleep, for the horse would bring master and cart surely home.

As a small girl, Lilian used to be allowed to ride on the horse as he left his cart and went down the lanes to his meadow. Once, arriving at a junction, she had a whim to turn left to the village post-office and get some sweets. But she could not get the horse to go this unauthorized way. He turned right as usual and safely brought her to his meadow, giving her a thought to last her lifetime. In Isaiah's country the carrying, pulling and ploughing were done by the ox and donkey, but it seems they were as faithful and wise as Lilian's horse.

Only today in the village, Bob, the energetic greengrocer,

was relating a wonder he had seen recently in Cornwall. His farmer friend went to open the gate for the large herd of cows that had already gathered there without being called. 'All he had to do was to open the gate. The cows sorted themselves out, each going to her own milking parlour where her own records were kept. All he had to do was to connect them to the milking machine. I'd like a job like that, I thought!' Bob's observation of animal wisdom was similar to Isaiah's, though his conclusion was somewhat different.

2

The Donkey: Humility and Glory

A donkey that saved her master

We love the patient dogs that are eyes to the blind or ears to the deaf. Touching also are the stories of animals that have given warning of deadly perils, as when cats or dogs insistently wake their owners because a fire has started. Recently in Birmingham firemen were puzzled when a dog did not run away from a blazing kitchen but remained there in distress – until they realized that an old lady lay on the floor within. Thanks to the dog, they were in time to save her.

The Bible has a story of a she-donkey which saved her master's life (Num. 22 – 24). It is bound up with epoch-making events. The massed tribes of Israel are pictured on the threshold of the Promised Land. From the mountains east of the Dead Sea, the king of Moab looked down on the encamped hosts and reckoned he would need supernatural help to withstand their might. In accordance with military practice of that time, he decided to summon a holy man to perform a ceremony of cursing the foe. He sent a delegation to a renowned seer in a neighbouring country with an urgent request for his services.

So it was that the prophet Balaam, after some hesitations, set forth on his journey to the land of Moab, riding the she-donkey on which he had ridden all his life. She did not know what great matters were in hand, or what important people were hurrying to and fro. But in her simplicity she proved to be more aware of God than was her master, the renowned holy man. For when the angel of the Lord came to bar his way, and stood with drawn sword in the road ahead, it was not the prophet who could see him, nor the two disciples, nor the princely emissaries from the king; it was the donkey. She alone saw the heavenly figure, God manifest, and from terrible danger she saved her master by swerving into a field.

The bewildered prophet struck her and sought to turn her back to the road. And now the angel barred the way between the stone walls of the vineyards. The donkey swerved and just got by, but banged her master's foot against the wall, and he struck her again. The way got narrower, and now the angel blocked it completely. But the donkey saved her master yet again by sinking to the ground. When he struck her again, the story continues, God gave her speech to remonstrate with him. Perhaps we would have called it body-language. At all events she was able to convey to him that her unprecedented behaviour had an urgent cause. We read:

Then the Lord uncovered the eyes of Balaam
and he saw the angel of the Lord
stationed in the way
with a drawn sword in his hand.
And he bowed down
With his face to the ground.

And the angel of the Lord said to him,
Why have you struck your donkey three times?
See, I came out as an adversary
for your journey was not pleasing to me
and the donkey saw me
and avoided me three times.

If she had not done so
you for sure I would have killed
and her I would have spared.

16

The penitent Balaam was then allowed to continue, on the understanding that in the great ritual ahead he was to pronounce only the words that God would give him.

And a great ritual it was. On a high place, in the presence of the king and princes of Moab, he offered sacrifices on seven altars and proclaimed the solemn words God gave him. This he did again from another high place. And yet a third time, from a mountain that gave him a view of all the ranks of Israel's tents below, he sang out the inspired words.

But alas for the king and his princes! The words he was given mounted to ever greater blessings on the pilgrim people. The power-filled poetry only prospered the in-comers and prepared the far-off days of victory for David and the mysterious royal star that would come forth from Jacob's descendants. From the first high place Balaam intoned:

> From the top of the crags I see them,
>   from the hills I espy them.
> Lo, a people that will dwell alone,
>   not reckoning themselves among the nations.
>
> Let me die the death of the righteous
>   and let my end be as good as theirs!

From the second summit, Mount Pisgah, he sang:

> See, I have been given blessing to impart,
>   for he will bless and I cannot turn it back.
> The Lord their God is with them
>   and in them will his kingdom be proclaimed.

And from the third height, in fullest inspiration, the seer sang these words over the hosts far below:

The oracle of one who hears the words of God,
   who sees vision from the Almighty,
      falling down with inner eye unveiled:

How fair your tents, O Jacob,
   your dwellings, O Israel!
Like broad well-watered valleys
   like gardens beside a river,
like aloes which the Lord has planted,
   like cedars by the waterside!

I see him but not as now,
   I behold him but not as near.
A Star makes procession from Jacob,
   a Sceptre from Israel.

And with many such words the Syrian prophet prepared the destiny of Israel and a ruler who would bring the light of God through the world's night. And so he mounted his donkey again and returned to his home.

Soon, from the same high mountains of Moab, Moses was to be granted his wide view of the Promised Land. And there in the mountains he would die. Long and hard had been his journey through the wilderness, but more than the view he was not allowed. But others led the entering in, and a time of victory was indeed to come for the tribes, and a time of royal empire, a time also when all would seem lost but the hope of the Star still to arise.

All this destiny our story has shown as based on mighty blessings given in oracles of ancient times, fate-shaping words given through a seer who owed his life and the successful outcome of his mission – to his donkey! She it was that could see the angel of God which the holy men and high officials could not see.

There is a further point in the story that ought to be mentioned. At the beginning the reader may be puzzled to note that God first authorized the prophet to make the journey, but then might have killed him for doing so. It seems as though two versions of the ancient story have been intertwined, giving rise to this contradiction. But the perplexing opening of the story that we now have has its value. We ourselves may have such an experience, where God opens a way for us, only to block it when we are in mid-course. Perhaps we are beginning to think of our own importance, or to listen too much to human voices. In such perplexities we may do well to sit quietly with an animal like the prophet's donkey, to imbibe some of her simplicity and innocence, and so be able to see God on our path.

The case of the disappearing donkeys

The idea that God might appoint an animal to serve him in some great purpose is fairly common in the Bible. In the story of Jonah, for example, God ordains not only a great fish (Jonah 1.17) but also a plant and a worm (4.6, 7) to counteract the perversity of the holy man.

In another story of epoch-making events, it is a herd of she-donkeys that God chooses for the launching of his action (I Sam. 9.1 – 10.16). There are various traditions about how the twelve tribes of Israel came to have their first king, a ruler anointed to be the holy Servant of God. In this particular story this great religious and political development is viewed positively, enthusiastically.

It all begins with the donkeys. Their owner, Kish of the tribe of Benjamin, was a man of substance, so the herd may have been quite large. How they came to get lost is not explained. Was pasturage hard to find? Were they disturbed by a wild beast or by cattle-thieves? We are only told that they were lost – and very difficult to find. Kish sent his son Saul and one of his servants to scour the

To imbibe some of her simplicity

surrounding territories. Over many hills and valleys they searched for three days without success.

They were tired and hungry, their provisions exhausted. 'Father will be worrying more about us than about the donkeys,' said Saul. 'We had better go back.' But it was when their errand seemed a failure that the turning point came. The knowledgeable servant pointed to a little town on a near-by hill and suggested consulting a renowned holy man who could be found there. The young Saul had not heard of the man, and though he thought the plan good, he wondered what present they could give the seer, now that all their bread was eaten. 'See', said the wise servant, 'I happen to have in my hand a quarter-shekel of silver, so I will give this to the man of God and he will advise us on our way.'

The town was one of those compact groups of flat-roofed stone buildings, crowning the hill and girt about with deep walls and gates. They began to mount the road leading up to it, when who should meet them on the way down but a band of happy girls, walking gracefully with water-jars on their heads or shoulders, on their way to the well.

Now Saul was an exceptionally good-looking young man, a head taller than most of his countrymen. When he asked if the seer was in the town, the girls seemed all to speak at once, and not with any simple 'yes' or 'no'. But eventually, loaded with advice and encouragement, the two made their way up to the gate.

At that very moment Samuel – for the seer was none other than he – was just coming out. Moreover, only the day before, the Lord had revealed to him that this meeting would occur. God was sending Saul to him, so that he should anoint him as royal ruler. It was a time of peril for the tribes of Israel. The highly efficient armies of the Philistines, incomers from a territory north of Greece, were pressing hard. Saul was to lead a better organized resistance. About the lost donkeys Samuel did not need to be told by Saul. He knew they had been lost, and in the meantime had been found. He told Saul and put his mind at ease.

Then he took the two along with him to the higher hill near the town, the place of worship. Sacrifice and feasting now took place there, with Saul treated as the most honoured guest, and one that the prophet had expected. Then they all went back to the town for the night, and Saul was given a bed on a roof – the spare bedroom of those flat-topped houses of few rooms, and no doubt the best place on a summer's night. Samuel called him at dawn, ostensibly so that the travellers could go far before the heat of the day.

In reality, Samuel had a private ceremony to perform before the town was astir. He poured oil on Saul's head, signifying that the Lord himself had anointed him and consecrated him to be ruler over the Lord's people. Samuel told him also of signs that would follow on the journey. Two men near Rachel's tomb would give him news that the donkeys were found. Then he would meet three pilgrims who would give him some of the loaves they were carrying up to the temple of Bethel. Finally, he would encounter a group of prophets playing instruments and moving and chanting in ecstasy, and he himself would be seized by the Spirit of the Lord and become a new man.

And as Saul parted from Samuel, so the story relates, God did indeed give him another heart, and all the signs came to pass that day.

Saul's appointment soon became an open reality. He proved to be a brave and in many ways a noble king. When he and his best sons were at last killed in battle with the Philistines, and his body was hung in mockery on the walls of Bethshan, there were faithful men who remembered what the young Saul had done to save them. They journeyed all through the night from across the Jordan, took down the body, carried it home for cremation and burial, and fasted seven days (I Sam. 30.8–13).

David and his dynasty supplanted the family of Saul, and the accounts of Saul's reign thus tended to concentrate on his failings in order to account for his death and his family's eclipse. But still, he was the first king of all Israel, the Lord's first royal, holy Servant. A foundation was laid which others were to build on. Saul played his part in preparing for David, and for David's Greater Son.

And the donkeys? Yes, our story gave them also a vital part. A mystery hangs over their getting lost and getting found. In neither case are we told the circumstances. It was all part of the mysterious working of God, who was leading Saul to Samuel and to the throne, and who prepared also all that Samuel had to do and the signs that would follow, on that wonderful day when the Lord's first Anointed was born again, filled with the spirit, and given a new heart.

It pleased the Lord to work his plan through the humble donkeys. They would not know that they were instrumental in saving Israel from the Philistines, in founding the kingdom, and in preparing for the far-off Messiah. But in their simplicity they did the will of the Lord. In his salvation the animals always have their part.

The prophecy of a messianic donkey

Tardebigge is one of those alluring places you never quite come to. You may follow the signposts which point to it along the lanes, but you never seem to arrive. But you do find several centres of interest which must be counted in Tardebigge. There is an old church with a tall spire crowning a hill. Below, you see a canal and tow-path, passing through thirty locks down into the deepening peace of Worcestershire's fields. A little higher up the canal you find a wharf with colourful barges for hire. In the meadows beside the wharf you see a dozen or more donkeys.

These donkeys are all therapists. People come to the Wharf Meadow to help look after them, to ride or walk them, or help others to ride or walk them. They come with special needs – physical or mental disadvantages, bad hearts, scars of human conflicts. Some even come on a doctor's prescription. From being with the donkeys they improve physically, mentally and spiritually. Having proved of immense value to their human owners for countless centuries, donkeys are being appreciated in new ways. These animals that have borne so many burdens, pulled the plough, so sure-footed, manoeuvrable, docile – these humble creatures are now seen to be agents of peace and healing. They are truly noble animals.

And in the Bible they appear also as much more than useful beasts. We have just seen their involvement in the introduction of sacred monarchy into Israel. And we had earlier noted the vital part played by Balaam's donkey in events which prepared royal empire for the tribes and hinted at a greater David beyond. To these royal and messianic connections of the humble donkey we must now add a famous prophecy of Zechariah (9.9–10).

The prophecy has the character of poetry that might have first taken shape in the days when the kings still reigned in Jerusalem, before the exile to Babylon in 586 BC. The ceremonies for beginning and renewing their reigns stressed the need for the ruler to have humility and faith; there are indications that he had to undergo symbolic sufferings before God's approval was signalled and he was clothed with symbols of salvation and declared 'right'. Then he would be brought from below Jerusalem's eastern wall to enter the holy city to glad acclaim, proved as humble, righteous and endowed with salvation.

Psalm 118 can be interpreted to reveal the outline of such a ceremony, with the king declaring:

The Lord chastized me sorely
  but he did not give me over to death.

Open to me the gates of righteousness,
  I will enter them and give thanks to the Lord.

I will praise you for you answered me
  and became my salvation.

His people reply:

The stone which the builders rejected
  has become the chief of the corner.

This is the day when the Lord has worked mightily.
  We will rejoice and be merry on it.

Blessed be he who enters by the name of the Lord!
  We have blessed you from the house of the Lord.

In such ceremonies a prophet might add winged words to draw out the meaning, showing what was intended by God for the particular occasion. Zechariah's poem seems to be such an utterance. It is a message of justice and peace that would know no bounds:

Rejoice greatly, fair Zion,
  Shout cries of triumph, Damsel Jerusalem!

See your king comes in to you,
  righteous and endowed with salvation,
humble and riding on a donkey,
  On a colt, a donkey's foal.

And he will remove war-chariots from Ephraim
  and war-horses from Jerusalem
and the war-bow shall be destroyed
  and he will decree peace for the nations.

And his rule will stretch from sea to sea
  and from the great river to the ends of the earth.

Of course, such poetry in the ceremonies was filled with
visionary ideals. The poet-prophets saw so deeply into the
nature of God's kingdom, that they spoke also for ages to
come, in effect for what was to be the time of the Messiah,
God's perfect age. Chapter 9 of Zechariah as a whole was
no doubt compiled when the kings had ceased to be and the
focus was on a future salvation. In this context, our little
fragment of poetry from the old royal ceremonies points all
the more easily to messianic days.

The donkey that fulfilled prophecy

The Gospels relate how Jesus solemnly entered Jerusalem in
the spirit of this prophecy (Mark 11.1–10; Matt. 21.1–11;
Luke 19.29–40). It is the entry we commemorate on Palm
Sunday. It was a significant part of that fateful journey
where Jesus had set his face to fulfil his mission in Jerusalem.

Mark relates how Jesus and his disciples approached the
Mount of Olives from the south-east side, having toiled up
the way through the wilderness from Jericho far below.
With prophetic sight, Jesus knew of the donkey ready for his
use and sent two disciples ahead to take loan of it, a colt
hitherto unridden. It may be that the donkey chosen for the
ceremonial entry of the ancient kings was also previously
unridden, having been consecrated for this sign of the new
reign under God. At all events, the significance of the taking
of this donkey was readily understood by the disciples and
by the throngs of Passover pilgrims.

The usual method for saddling a donkey was to place
several layers of thick cloth over the animal's back, then a
straw pad which was bound in place. A colourful rug might
then be laid over the pad and cloths. All this was improvised

for Jesus. Some laid their garments on the donkey's back, decking it regally for the joyous ceremony. Others laid their cloaks on the path, making it a royal and holy way. In symbol of life and salvation, green branches were carried or strewn in the way. Eastern crowds readily break into responsive songs and chants. Their words now drew on Psalm 118 and the thoughts of Zechariah:

> Save now!
> Blessed be he who comes by the name of the Lord!
> Blessed be the kingdom that comes,
>   the reign of our father David!
> Save now! (Shout it) in the heavens!

So the ancient vision of the Saviour-king had come to life. The new kingdom of God, channelled through his Anointed, had come to the threshold. But the elements of suffering and sacrifice, which the wisest of the ancients had always divined, were still entwined in the Saviour's way. His ride on the young donkey over the crest of the mountain overlooking the beautifully walled temple and city, and down through the eastern gate, was in reality a kind of transfiguration – an anticipatory disclosure of royal glory and peace before the battle with evil was joined.

In respect of the donkey, Matthew's account is distinctive. He tells of the colt being found with its mother, and of both animals being decked with garments and, it seems, ridden by Jesus. He quotes the prophecy of Zechariah and, disregarding the poetic style, has taken it to refer to two animals, colt and mother. The prophecy actually uses three expressions: 'donkey', 'colt', and 'son of she-donkeys'; but repetition is part of the Hebrew poetic style, and only one animal is intended.

But if Matthew's version arises from a rather wooden approach to ancient scripture, it may still show insight into

*The ancient vision of the Saviour-king
had come to life*

the ways of donkeys. The young colt might be expected to be found with its mother, and the company of its mother on its first ride would be a calming influence.

Meekness and majesty

Zechariah's prophecy of the entry of king and donkey began with a call for a joyous welcome. The prophet will have envisaged dancing and singing to the Lord. And he saw the joy as springing from the outbreak of peace. With the new reign of God through his Anointed, the weapons of war, the chariots and war-horses, were to be put away. God's ruler was to enter on the harmless donkey, a sign of peace and gentleness.

The horse was not a domestic animal in the oldest life of Israel, but after David's success in creating an important empire the horse-drawn chariot came to be adopted from other powerful states. Already David's son Absalom, ambitious for the throne, had got himself one, with a squadron of fifty men to run before him (II Sam. 15.1). But it was a younger son, Solomon, who succeeded David, and he developed armies of chariots on a grand scale. So the horse became a symbol of military might, and prophets like Zechariah foresaw its demise with the end of the pride of war, as the power of God's peace prevailed.

The harmless donkey was nevertheless a royal animal in some settings. In addition to its extremely useful function in general society, it had also in ancient Palestine a role of dignity. Some breeds indeed could approach the size of a thoroughbred horse. Such a fine donkey, decked with beautiful rug, could mark a noble rider. In the ancient prophecies of tribal destiny in Genesis 49, a ruler is imagined coming from the tribe of Judah, bringing harmony of nature; he is pictured tying his donkey to a vine, as he washes his garments in the abundant wine and drinks the flowing milk.

Of an early ruler it was said that he had thirty sons ruling thirty cities and riding thirty donkeys (Judg. 10.4). Another chief was said to have had seventy sons and grandsons riding their seventy donkeys (Judg. 12.14). A lame prince, son of Saul, was suspected by David of treacherous royal ambition when he rode his donkey in an hour of crisis (II Sam. 19.27).

From all this we can see that when Jesus rode into Jerusalem his action signified both peace and royalty – the dawn of God's kingdom. Humble, righteous and endowed with salvation, he rode an animal which was itself expressive of both meekness and majesty.

But perhaps we can go a step further than meekness *and* majesty. If today we contemplate such an animal with loving-kindness, we may be granted to know the majesty that is *in* meekness, the strength that is in vulnerability, the victory that is in innocence.

Mules and their burdens

An unspoken tribute to the donkey is perhaps to be found in Psalm 32. In contrast to the manageable donkey, the less familiar horse and mule seemed to the Israelites much more difficult to handle. Only with the use of bit and bridle and much skilful training could these more spirited animals be controlled for service.

This interesting psalm speaks first of the relief of facing up to one's sins, confessing them to the Lord, and receiving forgiveness. But it also teaches the importance of speaking further to the Lord, maintaining the relationship with requests and thanksgivings. Then in time of trouble you will find the Lord like a place to shelter in, like a high place of safety above swirling floods.

The psalmist speaks thankfully to the Lord (32.7), and what follows may be the answer he hears from God (32.8–

9). On this interpretation, the Lord undertakes to 'counsel' him, teaching and guiding him in the right way, looking into his eyes with the love of one deeply concerned for his welfare. Only he must not be like a horse or mule that needs restraining with bit and bridle to keep with its master. He must rather walk quietly with his Lord.

A mule results from crossing horse and donkey. It is fathered by a donkey and born of a mare. But it is sterile, so the crossing must be repeated for each mule. Consequently its role in old Israelite life was very limited, as was that of the horse. But it was potentially a very useful animal, combining the sure-footedness of the donkey with the strength of the horse.

Two such strong mules are mentioned as having unusual and very precious burdens in the enthralling story of the Syrian commander-in-chief (II Kings 5). It is a story full of divine surprises. The successful and greatly regarded general had contracted leprosy. The Israelite slave girl gave him good advice with all the earnest kindness of her heart. The great man followed it. He listened also to his servants when the rudeness of Elisha, typical of a holy man who tests out his visitors, nearly provoked him to give up. He humbled himself and was cured. And he asked for some Israelite soil to take home to Damascus, a quantity that two mules could carry for him. The earth was to form the floor of a shrine, where he would worship the God of Israel who had washed and healed him in the Jordan. So the mules, in their own way, were to spread the worship of the Lord.

Our feelings about the bonds of soil and worship are not as definite as those of Naaman's time, nor would the people of the Holy Land be pleased if all today's pilgrims took home mule-loads of their precious soil. But some have been glad to carry away a little water from the Jordan, perhaps for an infant baptism, and some treasure a pebble or two. In any case, there is much to carry home from the ancient story of a captive maid, a great commander who could be humble, a formidable prophet, and two sturdy mules.

The mule in a mysterious turn of fate

David's sons grew up as princes of a great empire. The animals they rode were mules, no doubt fine specimens, covered with regal hangings. And strange to say, in the long and exciting story of these sons and their struggle for pre-eminence, the mules play a decisive part.

After David's example, with acts of adultery and virtual murder (II Sam. 11 – 12), it is not surprising that some of the sons also abused their privileged status. The eldest, Amnon, committed a crime against his half-sister. He was murdered in revenge by the next son, the girl's full brother, Absalom, who took the opportunity to clear his own way to the throne. The murder was carefully planned and carried out at a great celebration of sheep-shearing, to which Absalom had invited all the princes. The first report reaching David was that Absolom had killed all the king's sons. David tore his garments and lay mourning on the earth.

But then the watchman saw a group of riders coming in haste over the mountain side. They were the king's sons, who had mounted their mules and fled back to Jerusalem. Among them may have been the young Solomon.

Absolom withdrew for a time to his grandfather's kingdom in Syria, but was later allowed to come home. Cleverly he completed his reconciliation to his father – and prepared a plan to usurp him. When the moment was ripe, he had himself proclaimed king with the general support of the population. David fled across the Jordan with his personal guards and there mustered what forces he could to face the hosts of Absalom. Though David's chances seemed slight, two unexpected turns of events sealed Absalom's fate.

The account of this dramatic history runs through many chapters (especially II Sam. 13 – 19). It is related with the greatest skill – a landmark in the world's literature. Unlike many other biblical narratives, this history says little directly of the actions of God. Rather as in our modern writings, it is the human actions which make the drama. But even so, God's justice and mercy are there, just below the surface.

The first surprising turn of events follows an earnest prayer of David. So Absalom amazingly disregards shrewd advice which would have brought him swift victory (16.31; 17.1–14).

The second decisive turn is not specifically linked to a prayer, but it was, at first, all that David must have longed and prayed for: Absalom captured but safe. As the battle raged through the forest, Absalom's royal mule ran under a great terebinth tree, Absalom was trapped in the branches, and the mule ran on. David's men saw him, but would not venture to harm him, in view of the king's instructions. Except for Joab. Well he knew Absalom's character and record, and what the outcome would be if he were spared. So he took responsibility for the killing of Absalom as he hung there.

We cannot say what would have happened if Absalom's hosts had won the day, or if the captured Absalom had been spared. We cannot imagine the succession without Solomon and Solomon's temple. But we can say that a miracle occurred, and that it came to pass through a mule.

3

The Marvel of Birds

A bird for a friend

Novice Margaret Mary was surprised before Sunday breakfast to see Sister Mary Alison, who was in good health,
grasping the bottle of brandy marked 'For heavy colds
only'. Indeed, all five nuns in the mission-house were
fighting fit, having just returned from early services in the
several churches to which they were attached. She was even
more intrigued to see that a drop of the brandy was for a
baby starling which Sister had brought home and put in a
box on the warm stove. A predator had attacked a nest in
the church belfry, and the fledgling had fallen straight down
the tower into the worship below. Sister had taken her up,
all the more encouraged by the Epistle read in the service:
'Every good gift and every perfect gift is from above, and
cometh down from the Father of lights.'

The young bird, now named Stella, perked up, and Sister
altered the label on the bottle to read: 'For heavy colds and
falls only'. Whenever Stella was hungry, she let it be known.
The nuns were kept very busy supplying her with
nourishment. During the nights she was entrusted to Novice
Margaret Mary, until the girl's eyes began to show signs of
oft-disturbed sleep. 'You must get a good night's sleep
tonight,' said Sister Mary Alison. 'I will have Stella in my
room.'

One of the novice's duties was to wake Sister in the

morning, as she was too deaf to hear the bell. But when she went in, she found Stella already on Sister's pillow, squawking in her ear and working hard to rouse her.

Some weeks later, Stella was accommodated in a shed where she could fly in and out. Whenever she saw Novice Margaret Mary walking outside, she would alight on her shoulder and sometimes creep under her big collar and wimple. Even from the top of factory chimneys beyond the bottom of the garden, or from a high gable in the street, Stella would swoop on to the black-draped figure, that must have resembled a large walking bird, and that just had to hope that the missile was none other than her winged friend. The two talked together and understood. 'You'll make me late,' said Margaret. 'You're always getting me into trouble.'

The time came when the mission-house was going to be closed and the nuns were preparing to move elsewhere. Novice Margaret Mary explained to Stella that the doctor was going to give her a home, and that his daughter was much looking forward to it. When the day came for the move, Stella was nowhere to be found. She was never seen again, and never forgotten.

Birds that helped Noah

Yes, many the stories that could be told of close bonds between birds and humans! A lady who rescues owls has a dozen or more at a time, and they respond to her love with trust and affection. And what a wonderful dimension has been added to the lives of coal-miners in north-east England by their love of pigeons! What a moment, on a day up from the coal-face, to see the flash of the bird's wings as it homed in from a flight of hundreds of miles!

Birds play an important part in the Bible's story of Noah and the flood. In a much older version written down by the

Babylonians, as the flood subsided and the boat came to ground on a high mountain, a dove was released, but it found no resting place and returned. Next, a swallow was sent out, and it likewise returned. But when a raven was released, the flood had so far receded that the bird splashed joyfully in the water, cawed loudly, and went its way.

This incident reflects a custom among sailors of the ancient world. We learn from Indian sources, stories of the Buddha from about 500 BC, that sailors would take a raven with them to sea. He would fly from the top of the mast and circle up to a great height, until able to detect distant land and make for it; otherwise he would return to the ship. Ancient Egyptian artists often depict birds on the mast of a ship, and Viking sea-farers are known to have made similar use of ravens.

The raven indeed is a robust bird, some twenty-five inches long, a master of flight. Though black all over, including beak and claws, it has a fine shimmer of blue-green and bronze. Tame ravens prove to be intelligent, companionable, and amusing.

The biblical version of the Flood has a similar incident where birds prove of service amidst the great waters (Gen. 8.6–12). It is a dramatic moment when Noah cautiously opens the hatch in the roof. Oh the light, the air! But his view is only of the sky, so he wisely turns for help to his friends the birds. In the present account, which has developed from various older forms of the story, the work of the raven seems to overlap with that of the dove, while the swallow of the Babylonian account is not mentioned. The greater prominence of the dove accords with the special importance of doves in the religious traditions of Syria and Palestine.

But it is still a thrilling part of the story. Noah puts out the trusty raven, strong and vociferous. It flies round about and returns, and does so a great many times, circling further and further, until at last the earth is dry enough for it to fly away. And Noah also sends out the dove, and her part is told in a climax of three stages. First, she finds nowhere to perch and quickly returns. How carefully Noah 'stretched forth his hand, and took her, and brought her in to him in the ark'. After seven days he sent her out a second time. All day she was gone, but in the evening-time, when birds customarily return to their nests, she came back to him – 'and behold, a fresh olive leaf in her mouth!' A third time, after another seven days, he sent her out again. She did not return, and so signalled to Noah that it was safe to strip back the roof and see for himself that all was well.

The dove with the leaf or twig of olive in her beak has since become a great symbol of peace, good news, and reconciliation. But we should also hear from her a message of the sympathy of birds and humans, and the possibilities of mutual help.

Some more messenger birds

The much-loved Coverdale translation of the Psalms has a breath-taking version of 68.13:

> Though ye have lien among the pots,
>   yet shall ye be as the wings of a dove,
> that is covered with silver wings,
>   and her feathers like gold.

There have been many interpretations of this psalm and this particular verse over the years, but it is probably best to see the dove once again as a messenger of peace. The ceremonies at Jerusalem's annual festival in the time of the kings were like a sacrament of God's reign. The ideal of his triumph over evil and his universal kingdom of peace was brought near in dramatic ritual. And Psalm 68 seems to

celebrate God's festal procession of victory back to his temple.

From an outlying place of ceremony, we may imagine, sacred doves were released to fly back to the temple in signal of the gospel of peace. In the early morning sunlight you would see the flash of their feathers – naturally iridescent, but perhaps also flecked with spangles of silver and gold for the great occasion:

> See, the dove's wings covered with silver,
>   her plumage gleaming with gold!

Such a ceremony would have some resemblance to a well-known practice of the ancient Egyptians. On their festal day they sent birds flying to the four compass points in proclamation of the divine sovereignty.

Another biblical passage about birds as messengers connects with a common English saying. 'How do you know that?', you may have asked when someone shows knowledge of a great secret of yours. 'Ah, a little bird has told me,' comes the teasing reply. You don't suppose a real bird could do such a thing, but people might have thought so in olden times. The wise ways of birds, their ability to fly, their speed and mobility, their gifts of eyesight and voice, their mimicry – all such features combined to get them a reputation for uncanny knowledge and ability to carry word. So the warning in Ecclesiastes 10.20 may have been understood literally; even if the reference is to spies, the image of birds may reflect a common belief:

> Even in your thoughts do not curse the king,
>   nor in your bed-chamber curse a wealthy man,
> for a bird may carry your voice,
>   yes, a winged one may spread the word.

39

Certainly there were accounts of birds that had brought offenders to justice. When the ninth-century Christian hermit Meginrat was murdered by two robbers, ravens he had reared flew after the guilty men, swooping on them, and filling the woods with such cries that the crime became known and the murderers caught.

Ravens that brought the bread of heaven

Ravens are the first birds to be mentioned in the Bible, and remain in the lime-light, even into the New Testament. They play an important part in the stories of Elijah (I Kings 17). The prophet was called to take a stand for the worship of the one true God at a time when powerful forces were promoting the worship of the nature-god Baal. To show that rain was in the gift of the Lord alone, Elijah had to announce a time of drought and then hide away in a ravine in the wilderness. There he was to drink from the Brook Kerith and eat bread and meat which ravens, at God's command, were to bring him morning and evening.

And so Elijah did, and was sustained by the friendship of the birds, until the brook dried up and God sent him to take lodging with a poor widow in the far north. There were to be times when Elijah felt that he alone was left to champion the cause of good against the rulers of the land (I Kings 19.14). But the Lord's forces were more numerous than Elijah supposed, and they included creatures like the ravens who received and obeyed the command of God.

In England's second city you may meet some remarkable individuals, often quite exotic. They seem to come suddenly over the horizon and quickly make friends. There was, for example, Sehdev, a kindly Indian sage, translator of Kabir; and there was his beautiful wife Aaloka, expert in Indian sacred dance. There was Solomon Raj, the artist I mentioned before, and his wife Mary who shared with a

group her skills of weaving. There was Cui-an, the quiet theological student from mainland China, a perfectionist in her work, now lecturing back in China. And then there was Chrissafina, a young Greek lady who was born near the Suez Canal.

Chrissafina was at first studying English preparatory to taking a course in art-restoration. But it soon became apparent that she was a well-trained, passionate, and brilliant painter of icons. At the end of her restoration course, before returning to Athens, she painted for us a really great icon of Elijah and the raven. She worked at it late into the nights, praying as icon-painters must, and putting her soul into it.

She shows Elijah in his thick red mantle, sitting at the mouth of a high, rocky cave beside the tumbling Brook Kerith. He is looking up at a raven that has alighted on top of a nearby rock, with food for Elijah in his beak. You could reflect for hours on Elijah's posture and expression and write pages on them. Above all, it is an expression of quiet wonder and love. He seems to contemplate his friend the raven, but also to look beyond to the faithful God who has sent the bird to his rescue.

The food which the raven holds in his beak is like a round, whitish wafer. So it brings to mind the manna in the wilderness, the bread of heaven (Ex. 16). Chrissafina has followed tradition for this scene, developed in centuries of experience and meditation. The follower of God moves in a wilderness, and is nourished only by what God gives, the bread of heaven. Marvellously, the animal world has its part in mediating that grace.

Jesus himself also noted how the ravens lived in the care of God (Luke 12.24). But when he speaks of humans having much more value than birds (Matt. 10.29, 31; Luke 12.6) we have to remember how he often taught with humorous and ironic touches. In the market place, the price of birds was much smaller than that for bonded servants or slaves. Jesus is ironically suggesting that his earthy-minded hearers should bear in mind that price-differential, and so accept that the God who provides for birds will also provide for them.

We have already noticed how stories abound of friendship between monks and wild creatures. In St Jerome's account of the very first Christian hermit, Paul of Thebes, a raven already plays a part. Jerome relates that another pioneer of the hermit life, Anthony, already over ninety years old, was guided to seek out his more remote predecessor in the solitary life. Through many hardships, he at length found the cave-dwelling of Paul, where a spring and a palm tree sustained the venerable hermit, who was now aged 113.

As the two sat together, a raven gently glided down and placed between them a whole loaf of bread. 'For sixty years,' said Paul, 'I have received a piece of bread every noon. Today, in honour of your arrival, Christ has doubled the ration for his soldiers.' But neither would take the honour of breaking the bread so, after hours of debate, they agreed each to pull from one end. St Jerome's enthralling story ends with the death of Paul and the devoted service of two lions, which scraped out a pit for the burial.

Such traditions are variations on the great theme: those close to God are close to the wild creatures. Trust is born, and friendship and mutual help abound.

Birds as images of the spiritual life

Feeling for wild creatures is revealed in the Bible's images drawn from wild life. Thus, when a psalmist wanted to express his dependence on God and his urgent need of him when he seemed absent, he compared himself to a fallow deer in a time of drought (Psalm 42.1; cf. Joel 1.20) The gentle creature wanders through the dry

43

wastes, stretching its head for the scent of water, as though imploring God.

It is often from the life of birds that such comparisons are drawn. A psalmist longed to escape from human strife to some remote place of peace, and he thought of a dove dwelling in the wilderness (55.6–8). In Coverdale's words:

> O that I had wings like a dove,
>   for then would I flee away and be at rest.
> Lo, then would I get me away far off
>   and remain in the wilderness.

It will be the rock-dove that is meant, the ancestor of our pigeons. It likes to nest on ledges of rocky heights deep in the wilderness. With long wings and swift flight, it can fetch food from great distances and then return to its remote home. Strictly vegetarian, it was for Jesus the image of one who is harmless (Matt. 10.16). There was a domesticated kind from very early times, which was used in sacrifices.

The dove provided an image for the Holy Spirit (Matt. 3.16). Indeed, a heavenly meaning had already been attached to the dove for thousands of years. Archaeology has recovered many depictions of doves associated with goddesses. It seems that the bird gave a sense of the heavenly realm and of communication between earth and heaven.

The worshipper longing to rest with God is also compared to the swallow that makes her nest in the structures about the temple courts (Ps. 84.1–3). In this most holy precinct, where none should do harm, she and her young will be safe:

> How lovely your abode, Lord of Hosts!
>   My soul pined and fainted for the courts of the Lord,
> my heart and all my body cried out for the living God.

Now my soul is a bird that has found its home,
    a swallow that builds a nest to lay her young
close by your altars, O Lord of Hosts,
    my king and my God.

It is indeed from birds that the psalms take their strongest figures for closeness to God. As the mother-bird covers her young protectively under her wings, so God promises to shelter his beloved. Thus Coverdale for Psalm 91.4:

He shall defend thee under his wings
    and thou shalt be safe under his feathers.

But in Psalm 17.8 the prayer for protection in the bosom of God uses two striking figures. There is again the image of the nestling under the mother's wing. But first comes the thought of the tiny reflection in someone's eye of a person standing close – that person seems to have entered the other's very soul and to be tenderly cherished. The psalm thus speaks for a suppliant in great distress who can nevertheless pray in hope of God's most tender love:

Keep me as the little one in your eye,
    hide me in the shelter of your wings.

The thought of the tiny reflection is combined with an even more remarkable comparison from bird life in Deuteronomy 32.10–11. This ancient poem tells how the Lord finds his people in the waste howling wilderness and takes them into his soul, as the tiny figure comes into the eye. And as a great bird of the wilderness (a *nesher* – it may be an eagle or a griffon vulture, with a wing-span of some eight feet) might hustle her young from the nest on some lofty cliff, hover over them, then float below them, ready to carry them on her wings as they learn to fly, so the Lord knows

45

our frailty in the fierce elements of life and is ready to bear us
up:

> He kept guard around them and cared for them,
>   he kept them like the little one in his eye.
> Like an eagle that stirs its nest
>   and hovers over its young,
> he spread out his wings and caught them,
>   he bore them up on his pinions.

Something similar comes in Exodus 19.4:

> And as on eagle's wings I carried you
>   and brought you to my dwelling.

Although such behaviour of eagles or vultures seems not
to be attested by experts today, we can believe that keen-
eyed shepherds, constantly wandering the wilderness, had
observed something of the kind. Our older commentaries
contain reports of such a sighting at Ben Weevis in Scotland,
where two parent eagles gave rest on their wings to their
young as they learnt to circle higher and higher.

Out in the wide wilderness which spreads about much of
the Holy Land, griffon vultures and eagles are a common
sight. They are skilled in using the moving air. They will rise
higher and higher in a rising spiral of warm air, and finally
glide down to begin again in another. They can float for
hours without effort, surveying the ground from a great
height. They can migrate over vast distances by simply
yielding themselves to thermal currents and winds. And so
the prophet of Isaiah 40 saw in them a parable for us. The
strongest of us, relying on our own effort, soon becomes
exhausted. But when we go trustingly with the Spirit-
breath, the Spirit-wind of God, we are borne up to swing
lightly on the Spirit's way:

He gives to the weary strength,
    and to the exhausted he gives great power.
When youths grow tired and weary
    and athletes stumble to a halt,
those who wait on the Lord are renewed in strength,
    they mount up on wings like eagles (*nesher*).

So Isaiah 40.29–31. The similar verse in Psalm 103.5 may refer also to renewal of plumage.

The wisdom of birds

The griffon vulture (*nesher*) is an object of wonder in Job 39.27–30. It is one of those creatures which live far from human control, and in their amazing skills arouse thoughts of the Creator who alone is their teacher. So high it nests, on some precarious tooth of rock! Yet from the height it can see its food down in the far distance. Also mentioned is the hawk (39.26), which arouses wonder by its migration. Only the Creator has taught it the wisdom of times and routes.

Birds indeed migrate in millions through the Holy Land, northwards in spring and southwards in autumn. Linking with the Nile Valley, the country forms an important part of a route which avoids the Sahara and the Mediterranean. It was astonishing to Jeremiah (8.7) that these birds knew from God their times and routes, while his people wilfully ignored his ordinances. Jeremiah mentions here the turtle-dove, which still moves north in masses every April, though some stay to breed. Its distinctive mellow voice characterizes spring days (Song of Songs 2.12).

Jeremiah also mentions the stork. Two kinds still pass through Palestine: the smaller black stork is solitary and rarer, while the white stork passes in thousands, a fine sight with its red beak and legs and its white and black plumage.

It may be seen flying with outstretched neck and trailing legs, or striding across fields and marshy ground. He may also mention the cranes, which pass over or spend the winter in the south of the country. This mostly vegetarian bird used to appear in flocks of thousands in the southern wilderness in spring, and some still stay to winter in communal roosts on the low hills near Beer Sheba. It has a wingspan of eight feet and stands about four feet tall, while its voice is something between a clang and a trumpet note.

The fourth migrant mentioned by Jeremiah is one especially familiar in Britain – the swallow. As we see them gather near summer's end for their immense journey, we may share Jeremiah's thought of the contrast with the human race, which readily forgets the times and ways of God.

The catalogue of wondrous creatures in Job also includes the largest of birds, the ostrich (39.13–18). It is between six and eight feet tall, and its wings are far too small for the heavy bird to achieve flight. Ostriches were to be found in the scrubby deserts of Palestine until around 1900. Their many eggs, with thick shells and up to eight inches long, are incubated mostly by the male. The hen will often cover them with warm sand and leave them for a while. When hunted, she may leave her young to draw the hunters away from them. Ostriches can run faster than a horse, maintaining 50 mph for half a mile. Some of these traits are reflected in the Job passage. Altogether, the ostrich seemed a puzzling bird to the ancients, but none could deny its gift of speed over the ground, and so the wonder of creation was again aroused.

Sympathy of birds and sufferers

There are birds which can give us a feeling of eeriness. If you were in a place of tombs in the night, and a solitary owl sat near you and hooted mournfully, you might well be disturbed by thoughts of death and the dead. All the more so if you knew the ancient idea that the souls of the dead might take the form of birds and linger near the corpse.

Something of this uncanny feeling is expressed in the lamenting prayer of Psalm 102.5–7. Coverdale's rendering has here a pelican, an owl, and a sparrow. But it is more likely that one bird is intended throughout, a kind of owl:

> Lord, hear my prayer
>> and let my cry enter before you.
> Hide not your face from me
>> on this hard day for me . . .
> for my days are burnt up in smoke
>> and my bones rage like a furnace . . .
>
> I am like an owl of the wilderness,
>> like an owl that dwells in the ruins.
> I watch sleepless like the solitary bird on a roof . . .
>> for you have taken me up and thrown me away.
> My days are as the last shadow of evening
>> and I am withered like dead grass.

It is a piteous prayer for help from one whose strength has been broken in mid-course (v. 23), and who is probably a representative spokesman for a broken community. It does not end without the thought of God's eternal being amid all change, and of his will at last to make all well.

There came a time when my late neighbour Lilian became sorely troubled. Above all, she suffered from severe anxieties and the confusion caused by the beginning of Alzheimer's disease. But she had one special comfort, a friendship that only she could appreciate in all its marvellous depth.

Her special friend was a robin. Every morning at breakfast time he would hop in through the open door and pick up the crumbs from the carpet, and this he did for several years. In addition to the endearing eye-contact, there was quite a lot of conversation between the two. It helped that Lilian could speak in tones quite like a robin's. Wherever she went in the garden, where she spent most of the day, the conversation continued.

It was just another example of the blessing that is passed from one species of creature to another when there is love. And all in all, we may say that the Bible's references to birds call us to a quietness and humility before the Creator, where the beauty, wisdom and friendship of birds can be known.

4

A Tapestry of Animals

Habitat in the Holy Land

Near the northern border of the Holy Land rises the mighty Mount Hermon, part of the truly mountainous terrain which stretches on through Lebanon. Travelling south, you are in a great rift valley, which gives first the marsh-lands of Huleh, then the fresh-water Lake of Galilee, then the valley of the River Jordan, then (well below sea-level) the highly salted Dead Sea, and finally a dry gorge running out to the Red Sea. If you remembered Mount Hermon for its snow, you would remember the later parts of your journey for their desert heat and for their surrounding cliffs and ravines.

Another memory would be the lush vegetation which the fresh water pouring from the great mountains produces in the warmth of the valley north and south of the Lake of Galilee. The River Jordan falls ever lower to its end in the lowest place on earth, and so passes into ever warmer regions. The flood-bed around its banks is therefore a dense tangle of vegetation, called in the old Bibles 'the pride of Jordan'.

We have been considering now only the thin strip descending from Hermon to the Red Sea, and I have said nothing of the main hill-country to its west, the higher lands to the east, the plain of Jezreel, the low broken hills of the Shephela, the shore-line of the Mediterranean, and the Negev desert. But already we can imagine the wealth of animal life in and around the Holy Land in biblical times. It is not surprising that the people of the Bible knew of lions and leopards, bears, hyenas, jackals and foxes, wild oxen and asses, deer, antelopes, camels, snakes, lizards, crocodiles. And we shall see that many such animals played quite a part in the prayers, praises and teachings of the biblical writers.

Lions that pray

Lions were widespread, and there are as many as 135 references to them in the Bible. When the Jordan flooded, they would be among the animals forced up from the thicket in the flood-bed (Jer. 49.19; 50.44), Living and hunting in family groups, and giving their oft-repeated roars, they came readily to the mind of Hebrew poets as images of fearsome foes, judgment, and majesty. Nahum compared the kings of Assyria to lions that had gone out and got much prey to feed their family (Nahum 3.11–12). Amos heard the Lord speak in judgment on various nations, including Israel; it was like the roar of the lion – how could a prophet ignore it (Amos 1.2; 3.3,8)?

The repeated roaring of the hunting lions, resounding through the night, seemed to the great poet of Psalm 104 to be the animals' prayer. In their need they were crying with a loud voice to God, asking for the supper that would suffice them for a few days (104.21). It is all part of this poet's vision of a world of myriad creatures depending on God. God's care for the hungry lions forms part also of the wondering contemplation of the natural world which comes in the climax of Job's experience, when he finds peace in God (Job 38.39–40).

A lion that faithfully carried out a mission for God features in a story in I Kings 13. The gist of the story is that a prophet from Judah crossed into the Northern Kingdom and delivered a threatening prophecy at Bethel, rather as the great Amos was to do in a later century. Declining food and drink, and setting off for home by a different route, he was so far faithful to his mission. But a Bethel prophet, no doubt much concerned about the prophecy of doom, decided to follow him and test its authenticity.

At first it seemed that the prophecy might be unauthentic, for the Judean was easily tricked into returning for a meal with the Bethel prophet. But on resuming his journey, the Judean was killed by a lion, which however did not harm the man's donkey, but stood guard over the body and donkey till the Bethel prophet came to the scene. It was concluded that the Lord had delivered the Judean to the lion, which had slain him according to the word of the Lord (13.26). This was taken as vindication of the original prophecy of doom, and the Judean prophet was given a tomb in Bethel as a mark of respect.

According to another story (II Kings 17.24–28) an uncommon occurrence of attacks by lions on humans was attributed to the fact that populations uprooted from afar had been forcibly settled in the area by the Assyrian conquerors, and did not know the requirements of the god of the land. It was as though they were not in harmony with the spiritual power of that territory, disrupted the balance, and so caused the aggression of the lions. The Assyrians took the point and sent an Israelite priest from exile to teach them the appropriate way of reverence.

A more familiar story of lions serving God is that of Daniel. Evil plotters had secured that Daniel be fastened into a den of captive lions. Guided by the angel of the Lord, the lions did not harm him. But when the plotters were made to take his place, the lions attacked them immediately (Dan. 6).

Less well know is the version in the Greek Bible (in 'Bel and the Dragon' in our Apocrypha). There are seven lions,

and their regular food has been stopped, and the ordeal lasts seven days; but the lions still do not harm him. Daniel's own hunger is miraculously relieved, for the prophet Habakkuk suddenly appears over the den with a bowl of stew and fragments of bread. This is particularly marvellous as Habakkuk had shortly before been on his way with the food to some reapers hundreds of miles away in Judea. An angel had told him to take it to Daniel, and when he protested his ignorance of the way to Babylon and the whereabouts of the den, the angel picked him up by his hair and blew him with a great blast all the way to the edge of the lion pit. He was returned home in like manner. Whether Daniel saved any of the pottage for the lions is not related.

Leopards in the forest and cats in church

The leopard generally keeps well away from humans, but it is distinctive enough to be well-known. Its spots gave rise to a saying of Jeremiah (13.23), who pessimistically concluded that there was as much hope that a leopard could change its markings as that the Israelites could change their conduct for the better, steeped as they were in a culture of callous behaviour.

Leopards abounded in the remote forests of the northern mountains, and the lovers of the Song of Songs imagined being together on the lofty summits of 'the mountains of the leopards' (4.8). Isaiah prophesied a world of peace, where the leopard would sleep beside a kid (11.6).

But when Habakkuk (1.5–10) foresaw warriors on horses 'swifter than leopards', stirred up by God to overthrow the Assyrian empire, he may have intended rather their swifter relatives the cheetahs. With longer legs and lighter build, the cheetah can sustain a tremendous speed for several miles, and was sometimes reared for hunting.

The small cats which prove such a great help and comfort in domestic life were common in ancient Egypt. They are pictured as helpers in the boats of fowlers in the marshes of the Nile delta, and no doubt were also invaluable protectors of the vital grain stores. It seems that it was only through the mediation of the Roman army that pet cats spread from Egypt through the Roman empire, including Britain. The lack of references to the small cat in the Bible is, however, not quite absolute. They make a brief appearance in the letter of Jeremiah in the Book of Baruch (6.22). This document of the Greek Bible (translated in our Apocrypha) is concerned to strengthen the faith of widely-scattered Jews by pouring scorn on heathen idols. These idol-gods, it says, have tongues polished by workmen and bodies overlaid with gold and silver, but are unable themselves to act or speak. Such gods cannot even save themselves from the accumulation of dust, nor from the ravages of moths and rust, beetles and candle-smoke. Moreover, from the dark spaces of the temples, bats and birds alight on the images, 'and in like manner cats also'.

This is curiously characteristic, for many a story could be told of modern cats that love to haunt the solemn spaces of churches and cathedrals. There was, for example, Orlando, who attached himself to the choir and staff of St Alban's Cathedral. At Matins and Evensong he was wont to occupy the bishop's throne. Outside our local church, two white Persians used to greet Sunday worshippers. For the quieter weekday services they would spirit themselves inside and suddenly manifest themselves on a high place, or signal their presence in a mysterious rippling of the altar frontal.

Dogs, foxes, jackals and hyenas

For domesticated dogs the biblical evidence is a little more ample. Small dogs under the table, ready to help clear up the children's crumbs, were well-known, at least just across the border in Phoenicia (Mark 7.28). An old lady used to tell me of the great service a poodle under the table did her in her Victorian childhood by helping her meet the strict requirements of eating everything served to her; it was particularly helpful in consuming daily an unpleasant milk drink considered essential to health.

Dogs are mentioned as working with the great flocks of sheep (Job 30.1) and as keeping guard. If overfed, a guard-dog might dream happily through danger and fail to bark – just like the self-indulgent leaders of ancient Jerusalem, who failed to give warnings about the stealthy advance of corruption (Isa. 56.10).

The love of dogs such as many modern people know is scarcely attested in the Bible, but there is just one incident in the Greek Bible (translated in our Apocrypha) which speaks volumes. In the Book of Tobit (5.16–6.2; 11.4) it is mentioned that when the young man Tobias set out on his long and adventurous journey, his dog went with him. And when he returned, having acquired a wife and much property and a cure for his blind father, his dog was still with him. Some versions develop the point a little and describe how the mother of Tobias, watching anxiously every day for her son's return and ready to tell her sightless husband, first saw the dog coming ahead. The Latin relates that the dog ran in advance and, coming up like a messenger, joyfully wagged his tail.

Foxes, jackals and hyenas are great survivors and can still be seen in the Holy Land today. The fox usually hunts alone at night and spends the hot day in his hole (Matt. 8.20). A smaller kind, pale and with large ears, lives in the deep desert.

Jackals are a similar size to the fox, but scavenge at night in packs. Some prophecies of ruin for cities include jackals in the portrayal of weird desolation (e.g. Jer. 49.33). The larger hyena is also a useful disposer of dead bodies, and his massive jaws are suitable for crunching large cattle bones. His uncanny howling laugh adds to the sense of desolation in ruined places, but allusions in the Bible are few and uncertain (e.g. Jer. 12.9, New English Bible).

Proverbs of ants, hyraxes, locusts, lizards and bears

It was said that God gave Solomon wisdom beyond measure and largeness of mind like the sand on the sea-shore. Three thousand were the proverbs he composed, and a thousand and five his songs. And the wisdom God gave him arose in his observation of trees and plants, beasts and birds, creeping things and fish (I Kings 4.29–34).

The Book of Proverbs preserves several wise sayings of this kind. The harvester ant was the object of much wonder. Its nest entrance is easily recognized, with trails of husks and well-worn paths leading up to it. What wisdom God has given this tiny creature to busy itself in spring and early summer collecting food to store under ground for leaner times ahead! Many a person would do well to go and watch it and imbibe some of its wisdom (Prov. 6.6–8)!

And there are things to see which are simply wonderful, arousing a spirit of awe, humility and worship. Of such is the vulture's way in the sky, rising effortlessly on spirals of hot air, gliding down from a great height; mysterious too the motion of the legless snake over rocks (Prov. 30.18–19).

A list of four small animals to wonder at includes the rock-hyraxes (where some English versions have 'coney' and others 'rock-badger'). About the size of a rabbit, these quaint creatures have round backs and no visible tail. They live on rocky slopes, where their flexible soles have a marvellous grip. Posting a sentry, they will sit at the mouth of a cave in dozens to warm themselves in the sun. Wonderful too are the locusts, which come quietly in orderly hosts, translucent in the sun, arriving and departing as one (Prov. 30.24–28).

The list just mentioned also includes the lizard – the rock-gecko. While residing in Old Jerusalem in the 1950s, I was always delighted to see any natural phenomena that linked with a biblical passage. All the same, I was a little startled, as I got into bed one night, to see a lizard about a foot long on the white wall immediately above the bed-head. It was beautifully spread on the smooth surface and had no difficulty in gripping the wall, and later the ceiling. They are equipped with rows of microscopic hairs under their toes, which can hold on to the smallest irregularities of a surface. This remarkable ability and their liking for stone-built houses are mentioned by the sage in his list of wonders – 'the lizard which takes hold with her hands and is in kings' palaces'. Such little creatures may well think nothing of human rank; in their perfection they can disdain it.

A proverbial expression for something really dangerous was 'a she-bear robbed of her young'. The Syrian bear was common on the mountains and hills, wherever there was wooded cover. The cubs weigh scarcely a pound at birth, as against the mother's five hundred pounds! These little ones follow her closely for several months, and it is no wonder she is especially solicitous for them. All the same, the sage thought it preferable to meet her when her cubs had been stolen than to meet a fool in full possession of his foolishness (Prov. 17.12). Of course, the 'fool' in Proverbs is a thoroughly wicked person, hardened against good values and apt to lead others astray. The bereaved bear as an image of acute danger was also used by a wise counsellor when he wished to play on the fears of David's enemies and spoil their strategem (II Sam. 17.8).

Bears normally avoid people, but, in the biblical view, they were as ready as other animals to carry out a mission.

When the ageing Elisha was sorely harrassed by a huge crowd of jeering boys, he invoked the name of the Lord against them, and two she-bears came out of the woods and rescued him, scarring forty-two boys (II Kings 2.23–24). The behaviour of the noisy gang may well have aroused the mother-bears, anxious for their young.

Swift and gracious: ibex, deer, gazelle and onager

Walking her dog in the mists of a Welsh moor, a lady recently had a remarkable experience with the wild ponies. She stood quietly among a group of ponies as one was beginning to give birth. While some ponies gently nuzzled her and her dog, the stallion comforted the heaving mother. The birth was completed in half an hour, and the mother lay recovering for another five minutes. Then she began to graze, while her foal spent an hour experimenting with standing, before achieving a wobbly stability. The whole experience made a deep impression on the lady, and in her subsequent walks the ponies have come to her as to a special friend.

Now in the catalogue of natural wonders set out so beautifully in Job 38–41 is included the birth of creatures of the wild – the ibex and the deer (39.1–4). Remote in the rocky wilderness, they owe nothing to man's wisdom, but are guided and watched over by God, who is their only midwife, knowing the time when the birth is due. The animal knows how to crouch and bring forth and set free the little one. With the care of God, the young gather strength, begin to run in the open country, and soon become independent.

The ibex, or wild goat of the mountains, is especially nimble on the desert cliffs and lives in groups of up to ten. Its splendid ridged horn can be as long as fifty inches in the male, remarkable for an animal that stands only some thirty-four inches at the shoulder. The deer is probably the fallow deer, which is about thirty-six inches tall, only the male having the characteristic antlers. Ibex and deer are again mentioned together in Proverbs 5.19, as figures of a graceful wife; the counsel is accordingly to appreciate her, love only her, and not go after loose women.

Especially swift and graceful is the gazelle, only some twenty-four inches high at the shoulder. Male and female have the characteristic pair of horns like the ouline of a lyre. The maiden in the Song of Songs (2.8, 9) imagines her lover coming to her over the mountains leaping like a gazelle. This passage breathes the air of springtime and has long been read at Easter time, with the thought of the risen Christ coming to his beloved and calling 'Arise, my love, my fair one, and come away!' The deer is added to the comparison (2.19), and is pictured again (as the female hind) in the triumphant conclusion of Habakkuk (3.19): through a present time of desolation, the prophet has won his way to confidence in the salvation of the Lord:

> But as for me, I will exult in the Lord,
>   I will rejoice in the God of my salvation.
> The Lord my God is my strength,
>   and he has made my feet like the feet of hinds,
> and over the high places he lets me bound.

Another wonder listed in the catalogue of Job is the wild ass or onager (39.5–8). With shorter ears than the donkey, the onager stands some forty-five inches high at the shoulder. Although a picture from Ur, about 2500 BC, shows onagers drawing four-wheeled chariots, they are known in the Bible for their wild freedom. Granted by God to run freely through the great spaces of wilderness and mountains, they can scorn the tumult of city streets and the shouts of drivers, which are the lot of donkeys.

Marvelling at the wild ox, horse and camel

A heavier animal of the wild, reputed for strength, was the wild ox, the aurochs. The bull stood six feet high at the shoulder. The reference to its magnificent independence of man in the Job list (39.9–12) mirrors the contrast with tame oxen, which pulled carts, ploughs and threshing sleds.

The horse appeared fairly late in Israelite history, and then mostly in warfare. Its strength and courage and eager energy are the subject of wonder in Job 39.19–25. Often the horse is mentioned as a symbol of sophisticated military might; such horse-power and the muscular legs of warriors cut no ice with the Lord (Ps. 147.10).

Yet a prophet foretold that when God's perfect kingdom came, the bells on the horses would bear the inscription 'Holy to the Lord' – the same as on the high-priest's head-dress when he went in to the Holy of Holies once a year. The prophet foresees a time when all life is so purified and renewed that all is in communion with the Lord. The priestly laws of holiness are no longer needed, and the presence of the Lord is reflected in all his creatures (Zech. 14.20).

Another remarkable animal, which does not feature in the Bible quite as much as might have been expected, is the camel. Palestine is not a habitat for wild camels, nor is it particularly suited to a settled life for domesticated camels. Furthermore, the widespread domestication of the camel seems to have been a relatively late development.

The genius of camels is their ability to carry loads through the great deserts, especially the Arabian. Their adaptation to that life is truly wonderful. Their hump provides a reserve of fat which can sustain them for a week or more without food or water. Their great nostrils close to a slit to filter out sand. Their eyes are protected by deep sockets and ample eye-lashes. Their mouths can cope with spiky shrubs, while their lips are delicate in picking leaves. The thoroughbred camel (the proper reference of 'dromedary') has longer legs and is much valued for riding and racing.

Camels feature in the stories of the semi-nomadic patriarchs, a beautiful example being Isaac's marriage to Rebekah (Genesis 24). The senior steward of Abraham's household has been sent from Palestine to northern Iraq to seek out a wife for the only son Isaac from among Abraham's kinsfolk. He has taken ten camels carrying gifts, and has reached the well outside the town of Nahor. It is evening, and the girls and women have come out to fetch water in the jars which they carry gracefully on their shoulders.

The steward has his camels kneel down beside the well and prays to the Lord for guidance – 'Let the damsel to whom I shall say, Pray, let down your jar that I may drink, and who replies, Drink, and I will give your camels drink also, let her be the one whom you have appointed for your servant Isaac.'

Hardly had he finished his prayer when Rebekah came out with her jar on her shoulder, a beautiful girl:

> She went down to the well and filled her jar and came up. And the steward ran to meet her and said, Pray, give me a little to drink from your jar. And she said, Drink, sir. And she at once let down her jar upon her hand and gave him drink.

The skilful story-teller has won our hearts for Rebekah, but for the moment left the crucial issue open. But then he continues:

> And when she had done giving him drink, she said, I will draw for your camels also, until they have done drinking. And she hurried and emptied her jar into the

trough, and ran again to the well to draw, and drew for all his camels.

And so she continued until the camels were satisfied, and all the while the steward watched her intently, silently seeking the Lord's confirmation. As the tale progresses, Rebekah's brother Laban proves to be equally attentive to the camels, preparing them a place, ungirding them, and giving them straw and provender.

Guided by the Lord, the steward's negotiations go well, even to the vital point as to whether the prospective bride will herself consent to leave her home for Palestine, rather than require Isaac to join her. Solemnly she attests, 'I will go,' and the contract is completed.

The camels are in at the happy conclusion. In the southern wilderness, the Negev, Isaac has walked some way from his tent, meditating as evening draws on. Wondering what is to come for him at this crisis in his life, he strains his eyes to the horizon, and suddenly he can make out the approaching camels. Rebekah too is on the watch:

And she lifted up her eyes, and when she saw Isaac she slipped swiftly from the camel. And she said to the steward, 'What man is this who walks across the plain to meet us?' And the steward said, 'It is my master.' So she took her veil and covered herself.

The marriage was consummated without delay, and Isaac greatly loved Rebekah, and was comforted for the death of his mother.

Now in this idyllic story great stress is put on the seeking of the Lord's guidance and the response of the Lord's faithful love. In Isaac is concentrated all the promise and hope of the Abraham stories – the future of God's work of blessing for a people and for the world. Vital is the rightness of the marriage, and the sign of the right bride was her kindness to a traveller and his animals. Camels can indeed go long without drink and food, but the good owner fed and watered them daily and took great care of them. Rebekah made light of the task of repeatedly going down to the well and climbing up again with the heavy jar to replenish the trough for the ten thirsty camels, and her brother too made every provision for their care. The steward would not himself eat until he had explained his mission, but even before that the camels must be ungirded and provided with straw and provender for the night.

The sign which the steward asked of God was well judged. He did not request some irrelevant or miraculous circumstance, but he asked for a sign of a truly kind heart, and the sign was fulfilled in Rebekah. She became the agent of God's own kindness (24.14).

Children called Snake, Flea and Bee

We have already noticed the wise man's wonder at the motion of a snake over rock. Other references to snakes usually reflect the fear which the poisonous fangs of a few species cause, though in fact many species are harmless to man. We have seen that the snake in Genesis 3 has a mythical quality – an extraordinarily shrewd creature, representing here the experience of temptation. The poisonous bite of some snakes is compared in Psalm 140.3 to the wounding tongue of the wicked. In Psalm 58.3–5 the speech of the wicked is again compared to a snake's venom, while their deafness to good counsel is compared to the deafness which is in fact found in all snakes, though they are sensitive to vibrations.

The curious tale of signs and magic in Exodus 7.8–13, where staffs are changed into snakes, and some are swallowed by others, has been thought to have some connection with a trick of snake-charmers. They can hold a cobra suspended from its neck and induce temporary rigidity. It is also the case that cobras sometimes swallow other species.

But the prophet Isaiah (11.8) brings us to a happier picture, since in his vision of the messianic time little children can play safely over the hole of the cobras and over the nest of the vipers. All are friends, and the enmity of the age of estrangement (Gen. 3.15) has been overcome.

It may seem surprising that parents should name their child 'Snake' (Nahash), but the name occurs several times (I Sam. 11.1–2; II Sam. 17.25, 27). We find that other parents gave the name Flea (Parosh), others Dog (Caleb), others Bee (Deborah). In the important story of II Kings 22 we meet an official called Rock-Hyrax (Shaphan), another called Mouse or Rat (Achbor) and the prophetess Weasel (Huldah). Elsewhere and more familiar is the lady called Ewe (Rachel) and the prophet Dove (Jonah).

In the main Old Testament period it was not the practice to name a child after some relative, let alone to choose a name (as we sometimes do) for its sound, without a lively sense of its meaning. The name, often given by the mother at birth, expressed a deliberate thought in the present common language. The likelihood is that in most of the names just quoted the idea was to repel, to make the child unattractive to demons, spell-makers, evil eyes; the message was that this child stings like a bee, bites like a snake or a dog etc. An Arab saying was that 'we name our camels for ourselves, and our children for our enemies'.

Two mystery beasts: Behemoth and Leviathan

'Behemoth' might be translated 'the great beast' and is described near the end of God's speech depicting animals (Job 40.15–24) What can it be? Mighty are his muscles and limbs. He was made at the outset of creation and only the Creator can control him. He lives contentedly. The mountains provide crops for him and wild creatures play happily about him. He loves to lie in the shade of lotus trees, among the cool reeds of the marshlands or the poplars of the brook. He copes easily with the flooding of the river or assaults from hunters.

'Leviathan' probably means 'the Twisting One' and is described at length as the last item in God's catalogue of natural wonders (Job 41.1–34). God speaks with admiration: 'I will not keep silence over his limbs nor over his strength and the grace of his build.' Leviathan is armour-plated with rows of shields, joined exactly so that nothing can penetrate. When he sneezes, lights flash and his eyes glow red. From his nostrils stream smoke and flame. As befits the king of beasts, an angel of glory sits on his neck and an angel of dread goes before him. Hard are the folds of his flesh, and hard as a millstone is his strong heart. Heroes flee at his stirring, for to him all weapons are but straw. His lower scales cut the ground like the teeth of a threshing sledge. His tail lashes the deep into froth as on an ointment-pan, and behind him stretches a foaming wake.

Two remarkable creatures indeed, and various identifications have been suggested. Elephants, buffaloes, dolphins and whales have entered the competition, but the favourites have been the hippopotamus for Behemoth and the crocodile for Leviathan. These two animals have indeed probably contributed most to the depictions, but can hardly be the complete explanation.

Rather, the poet will have had in mind the monsters which traditionally symbolized chaos. The Creator's work at the birth of the universe was often pictured as the overcoming of such monsters. In subduing them – such was the story's meaning – God brought from the chaos a world of order, life, and beauty.

In Job the monsters are not presented negatively as horrible apparitions. Rather, they arouse wonder and admiration, and God takes pleasure in them. The meaning is that even the forces of chaos become transformed by the work of God and share in the peace and beauty of his creation. Contemplation of Behemoth and Leviathan – chaos transformed – arouses awe at all that creation has involved and at the unique and powerful wisdom of God, from the time before time began down to the present life of the cosmos, and on to the completion known only to the intuitions of the heart.

And those who with kindness rescue living things, wresting from cruel powers a little world of peace, are children of the Creator, following his pattern. However much the cruel enemy swells over them, their transforming work is never overcome or blotted out. It will form part of the joyful final transformation.

Near Tardebigge you can meet an enormous pig called Lucy. Though mighty in muscle and limb, she has no lotus trees to give her shade, nor reed-beds, nor poplars of the brook. But she lives contentedly in the grassy paddocks, and round her play lambs and goats and ponies. Her sneezes do not set lights flashing, nor do her eyes glow red, but she has the strength to push over a hen house in her passion for eggs, and many have admired the grace of her build. If you go through the gate of the Farm Animal Sanctuary, past the friendly dogs, she will come to greet you and will walk with you contentedly.

As a tiny piglet she was found under a hedge five days after her pig unit had been burnt down with the death of all two hundred pigs. A few days later she was brought to Janet at the Sanctuary. On her back are still marks from the fire, but she is happy in that little kingdom of compassion. You have to feel better when she nudges you or looks at you with trust.

Wresting from cruel powers a little world of peace

On the wall of a rock-tomb in Amarna, Egypt, was found a hymn in praise of the 'Aton' – the Creator revealed in the sun-disk. It was composed about 1370 BC, and is a beautiful expression of sensitivity to the life of nature and the divine light and care.

The daily rising of the sun is seen as a time of joy. Washing and dressing, the people raise their hands in praise and gladly begin work. Beasts go happily to their pastures, trees and plants flourish anew, and birds give praise as they glide on outstretched wings. Boats set out up or down the great River Nile. Fish dart before the bright face of God, whose rays shine into the green waters.

The hymn then mentions the night, which brings a contrast. The face of the Creator is no longer radiant over his world. It is a time of danger, when thieves are abroad, lions hunt and creeping things may bite or sting. How welcome again will be the morning, when God's bright rays suckle every meadow, and life abounds!

But the Egyptian hymn sees the work of God also in the dark mystery of the womb. There the Creator soothes the unborn child and stills its weeping – 'thou nurse already in the womb!' And a chick in its shell is marvellously given breath by God, who hears its call. And God tells it when to break the shell and come forth to cheep and walk.

Centuries later something of this poetry lives on in what had once been an outpost of Egyptian empire – Jerusalem. So we have the beautiful Psalm 104, which adapts the tradition and re-creates it in the manner of Israelite faith.

The psalm expresses communion with the glorious Creator. Thoughts of winds, springs, plants and animals do not distract from the communion, but intensify it. The worshipper adores the Lord whose creative wisdom and unceasing care are seen in all the living world. As the natural elements and the animals are recollected and described, the reality of God shines all the stronger.

In the first part (104.1–10) we hear of the Creator's preparation of the earth for life. The poet imagines how the Creator subdued and disposed of the mighty waters and secured a firm earth. In the next part we hear of the creatures which now enjoy the life God has so marvellously provided and watched over. First are mentioned the wild animals that drink from the brooks, and the wonderfully free onagers (wild asses) are especially named. Trees abound by the streams, and here live the birds in all their varieties, singing their hearts out. From the gift of rain comes the grass and vegetation, provided for cattle and for man. On the great mountains are the forests and giant cedar trees. Here again are many birds, but most conspicuous in the fir trees are the huge nests of the storks.

The psalmist reflects how for each creature there is a suitable home. How the ibex (wild goat) can leap over the craggy mountains! How the rock-hyrax loves the cavities and stones of the mountain slopes!

Order and beauty mark the alternation of day and night. With the high processions of sun and moon comes in its turn the night, which serves the animals of the forest that creep forth in its cover. Especially noted are the hunting lions, and their repeated roars are taken to be calls to God for their food. When the creatures of the night hide again for their rest, it is man's turn to come forth with the sun and enjoy working through the daylight hours. And this reflection on the variety and fitness of life on the land ends with an exclamation of praise to the Creator:

> O Lord, how manifold are your works!
>   In wisdom have you made them all,
>   the earth is filled with your creations.

BLESS THE LORD, O MY SOUL! O LORD MY GOD, YOU ARE VERY

GREAT, YOU ARE CLOTHED WITH HONOUR & MAJESTY

YOUR SPRINGS GIVE DRINK TO EVERY WILD CREATURE

THE WILD ASSES QUENCH THEIR THIRST, BY THE BROOKS

NEST THE BIRDS OF THE HEAVENS, THEY SING AMONG THE BRANCHES

YOU GIVE DRINK TO THE MOUNTAINS FROM YOUR STORES ABOVE

EARTH'S NEED IS SATISFIED BY THE FRUIT OF YOUR WORKS

MY GOD, YOU ARE VERY GREAT — BLESS THE LORD, O MY SOUL

And then thought turns to the sea, 'great and wide, wherein are things creeping innumerable'. Here travel the ships, in a wonderful interplay of the elements. And the sailors glimpse Leviathan; distant sight of a whale or other great sea creature suggests the monster of chaos which the Creator transformed and tamed into a playful friend.

All on earth and in the sea depend on the Lord. By his breath they live. And to this Lord our poet would sing as long as he has any being. Then he adds a concluding prayer that the wicked be consumed out of the earth.

No one who has reckoned with the evil which man has wreaked on animals, trees and waters could think this prayer superfluous. It is not out of harmony with the beautiful psalm, but an essential part. Whatever further action has to be taken to counter the destructive evils, wholehearted prayer against them is fundamental. In our hearts today the prayer should be that the spoilers should be brought to the end of their existence *as spoilers*, and reborn as carers, humble before God. But certainly the death of cruelty and ruthlessness, in them and in ourselves, should be our constant prayer as we contemplate the beautiful mandala of life that is God's world.

5

The Lamb and the Throne

Lambs loving and loved

A spindly dog trotted along the road, turned into the shopping street, carefully crossed over, and made for the doorway of M. and J. Dancer, Family Butcher. He tapped and gave a short bark. He was promptly admitted, and soon re-emerged carrying a large bone, and trotted back home. He was a regular visitor, and but one of the many animals and people that benefited from the alert kindness of the Dancers. On the ground behind the shop they had ducks, poultry, ponies and hand-reared lambs.

Despite their name, the Dancers were a sturdy family. During lulls in trade, Michael Dancer's ample form would fill the doorway, as he took note of comings and goings in the village and enquired after the welfare of passers-by. He needed no 'inter-com' to communicate with his wife Janette if she was somewhere above or behind the shop. He would call to her in stentorian tones.

'Janette!' he bellowed into the back hall one day when I called to give him exciting news. 'Janette!' He tried with more success through the back door, adding a summary of my news. There was a sound of running feet. Janette burst in breathless, slammed the door and leaned hard against it, bright-eyed and laughing. What on earth had pursued her?

'It's those lambs,' she said. 'I have to feed them at the far end of the ground and then run like mad to stop them getting into the house with me.'

It was a dramatic illustration of the way lambs get attached to those who rear them. At the Farm Animal Sanctuary Janet Taylor cares for many lambs, left with her in sickly condition, nursed and given a life of peace. Each one has its own character and will ever be remembered for some example of high spirits or affection.

One indeed was aptly named 'Spirit'. Blind from birth, he has brought his own contribution of happiness to the world. A very old lady was moved to write a poem about Spirit. She pictures the scene outside the barn on a sunny morning, as we call his name, and the blind lamb comes bucking and jumping in sheer joy of living. We watch him with tears and are moved by love to be better people.

And here we touch a mystery of tenderness which is perhaps as old as the world. When King David had done a great wrong, so we read in II Samuel 12, the Lord sent the prophet Nathan to him. How should the prophet speak to this battle-hardened king, realistic ruler of an empire – how penetrate to his conscience? Nathan spoke what the Lord had given him: the story of a lamb.

He told of a poor man who owned nothing but one ewe lamb. The man reared her and she grew up in the house with him and his children. Of his own morsel of food she would eat, from his own cup she would drink. She would lie in his bosom and was like a daughter to him. But one day a man rich and mean seized her, killed her, and served her to his guest.

Hearing this, David was moved to anger. 'As the Lord lives,' he swore, 'the man that did that shall surely die . . . because he had no pity.' And the prophet replied, 'You are that man,' and he explained that his story of the lamb was a parable of the king's own crime. David accepted the prophet's condemnation and took the hard way of repentance, and so was just able to bear the many sorrows which his conduct had set in train.

The Lord my shepherd

The traditions of Israel's greatest king portray him as having in his youth shepherded his father's sheep. There David learnt the bond of man and animal. There he more than once risked his life to save a lamb, as he faced lions and the dread Syrian bear with his simple weapons (I Sam. 17.34–5).

He is portrayed also as a man of poetry and music, with deep feeling for God. And of all the prayers and praises collected under his name, the best known still today is the shepherd song, Psalm 23. It is loved for its peaceful imagery from the open country. It is loved for the light that the bond of shepherd and sheep throws on God's care for us. And most precious is the assurance that his care continues through the dark valley of death until we come home to him for ever.

Some readers trace the figure of the sheep right through the psalm, and so they trace the thought somewhat as follows. Because the sheep has a good shepherd it does not suffer from hunger. In the rocky hills and round the edges of the dry wilderness the shepherd knows where green pasture can be found for peaceful grazing and rest. Scarce as water is, he can find the still pools near a well or held in the tumbled rocks of a wadi. In all the broken, mountainous country he knows the right way and leads his flock faithfully as a matter of honour. Through the dark ravine, where robbers or predators may lurk, he guards his sheep with his club and guides them with his crook. Whatever dangers are near, he will get his sheep to a table land, a good level pasture. And there he will treat the injured with oil. Followed by the protecting sheep dogs, the flock returns to the fold, where the shepherd is also at home, never leaving them.

Other readers agree for the first part, but in 23.5–6 think the figure has changed to that of the good host and his guest. The table is bountiful, and the custom of anointing the head with oil on festive occasions gives comfort and cheer.

There is, however, another dimension of the psalm which should not be overlooked. Shepherd and flock had been symbols of God, king and society for thousands of years in the Near East, and continued to be so in Israel. The words and thoughts of this great psalm are therefore permeated with the idea of God as heavenly king who orders and blesses society through his chosen representative, his 'Anointed', and through the temple.

Bearing all this is mind, we can hear further echoes in the familiar phrases. The 'paths of righteousness' suggest the processional ascents to the temple, where the salvation of God was celebrated at the annual festivals. The 'rod and staff' evoke the symbols of God's rule, like the sceptre and crook still used in ceremony today. The 'table' prepared 'in the sight of foes' is a symbol of covenant, as archaeology has shown: God gives open notice that this beloved one is under his special protection. The 'goodness and mercy' are the personified qualities of his reign, such as were symbolized by animal figures at the base of thrones. The 'house of the Lord' is the Jerusalem sanctuary, beside which lived the anointed and sacred ruler, the royal Servant of the Lord.

Seen in this way, the psalm is even richer than generally supposed. For David, or for one who should follow him in his high calling, it expresses profound confidence in the king of all existence, who has undertaken loving care of him. God gives to his Anointed victory over death, life for ever in his presence. And all who take up this song in faith can enter the same bond, for the Anointed, God's lamb, seen fully in Christ, is also a good shepherd to us. Through him, with him, we too can come to the still waters, pass through the valley of the shadow of death, and abide for ever in the eternal Presence.

The lambs in God's arms

God as both king and shepherd is also the subject of a thrilling vision in the Book of Isaiah (40.9–11). Again there is reflection of the great festal processions which signified the entry of God with salvation. But the prophet and his first hearers were far from Jerusalem, which indeed lay in ruins. To his fellow exiles by the waters of Babylon the prophet is announcing a time of forgiveness and return, salvation and new life. Drawing on memories of the celebrations before the Exile, he projects a tremendous scene in the imagination.

A highway, a holy way is prepared through the wilderness, with levelling of hills and filling of holes. From the eastern desert it leads up to the holy city. Messengers go ahead to carry the good tidings of the divine victory and deliverance. Then:

> Behold, the Lord God comes in with might,
>   his arm having proved victorious!
> Behold, the spoils of victory with him,
>   and before him what his deeds have won!
>
> As shepherd, he shepherds his flock
>   and in his arm he gathers the lambs
> and carries them in his bosom
>   and leads to water the ewes that give suck.

So the prophet conveyed to his broken people his overwhelming conviction of the divine power and love. God is king and shepherd, conqueror and sacrificial carer. It would not be an easy message to convey in the refugee camps of today, some of them also fifty years old. But there is a moment when to the deep-seeing eye the heavy curtains of suffering part, and the light of a greater reality shines out.

Perhaps we know something of that deep vision when we behold a lamb, or some other defenceless creature, and have compassion. We have touched the fringes of ultimate truth, the reality which is supreme and enduring.

An offering to the Lord

If the shepherd is a sacrificial carer, it seems there is a circle of sacrifice. In the religion of ancient Israel, lambs and sheep were prominent among the animals killed at the sanctuary as offerings to God, and in some cases consumed partly by the worshippers in meals of sacred fellowship. The accounts of the regulation and practice of such sacrifice are not easy to follow, as the practices of many shrines and periods left fragments of record to add to the accumulation. Nor is there given any adequate philosophy of sacrifice. We have to recognize that here is something rooted in remote pre-historic times, adapted to later situations, a thing of instinct and intuition, symbolism and tradition. It will yield more meaning to poets than to lawyers.

In chapter 1 above, we noted that the custom of sacrifice marked the solemnity of an animal's death. All was done in obedience to the Creator's laws and before his face. Even when animals were killed away from the sanctuary in later centuries, the careful pouring away of the blood respected the sacredness of the creature's life.

Other themes can be discerned. The first-born, like the first-fruits of crops, was sacrificed to God to witness that all was his, and only with acknowledgment of his sovereignty could further off-spring be taken for human use.

Other animals might be sacrificed in ceremonies of thanksgiving. In a time of need a prayer had been made with a vow of sacrifice, and now acknowledgment was made of answered prayer by fulfilment of the vow and by words of testimony.

When a meal took place at the sanctuary, with part of the animal symbolically made over to God and part consumed by the worshippers, there was the thought of 'peace'. A relationship of trust and friendship was renewed between God and people.

Some sacrifices were described as sin-offerings, making atonement for wrongs, bringing reconciliation with God. Of these some priestly traditions stated that their effectiveness was limited to the cleansing of unwitting errors. For sins committed 'with a high hand' a penitent could only throw himself on God's mercy.

The outstanding example of the sacrifice of lambs was for Passover. The story expressing the meaning of this observance is found in Exodus 12. By divine command the slave-people were to kill a lamb in each family. With a spray of hyssop they were then to put some of the blood on the door-posts and lintels of their houses. The lamb was to be roasted and wholly consumed that night, with the family being all prepared for hasty departure. Angels of death were to pass through the land, killing all first-born of man and beast, but where they saw the lamb's blood on the door-ways they would spare and pass over. So the oppressor people would at last be forced to let the enslaved Hebrews go out to their journey through the desert to freedom.

The blood of the lamb, the essence of its innocent life, thus guarded the people from death and enabled them to go free to new life with God.

An animal not to be overlooked: the goat

At the very end of a rising garden in St Blazey, Cornwall, is an old stone wall. On the far side leans a hut which is the night-quarters of the neighbour's pretty goat, Lucy. From her height on the rising ground, she often gazes down into the garden intensely, no doubt noting all the excellent shrubs and shoots which no one is eating. One afternoon the neighbour, Lionel, was calling anxiously for Lucy. There was no sign of her all up the hillside. He was really distressed.

Then he heard a bleat, and to his relief and delight he found her in her night quarters. Normally he has difficulty every evening in enticing her into the hut, but this spring afternoon she had found the north-east wind unpleasant and had surprised him by bedding down. It was clear that for Lionel his goat was as lovable as any lamb.

The instructions for the selection of the Passover lamb state, 'You shall take it from the sheep or from the goats' (Ex. 12.6). Goats in fact were usually kept with sheep, a unity of 'small cattle'. A common Hebrew word for 'flock' (*son*) means sheep, goats, or both together, and a common word for an animal from the flock (*se*) could apply equally to a sheep or a goat. In our imagination of Psalm 23, the Passover, and many other bibilical scenes, we are inclined to think only of sheep and not give the goats their due honour.

There is, however, one famous biblical scene where it is definitely the goat which seizes our attention and arouses our wonder and pity – the scapegoat of Leviticus 16. In that chapter it is described how on the tenth day of the seventh lunar month (September or October) there was to be strict fasting and no work. On this day the high priest performed the annual ceremony of atonement. The theme was the putting away of all the past year's sins, so that the new year begun about this time could see a new start with God.

The priest's task was fraught with danger as, for once in the year, he went right up to the symbolized Presence of God in all its dread holiness. The priest's survival, it was believed, depended on his obedience to the prescriptions received from God, in which a crucial part was played by the offering of animals. The innocent life of these creatures stood between the priest and instant death, and between the people and fatal disaster.

The animals brought forward included a bull-calf and two male goats. The priest killed the calf and one of the goats, and with the blood of each in turn touched the symbols of God's Presence and the altar seven times. Thereby he made peace for any harm that might arise there from the unworthiness of himself and of the people. Which of the two goats was to be killed had been decided as the animals stood before the holy symbols by casting lots. Through this method, it was believed, God's choice was expressed.

The goat chosen to live was the scapegoat: it was appointed to carry away all the people's sins of the old year. The chief priest placed his hands on the animal's head and confessed the sins on behalf of the people. All the sin and guilt were thus considered to be loaded upon the goat, itself innocent and perfect of its kind. A specially appointed man then led the goat into the wilderness, to some place where a rocky gorge would bar its return. The man would take all precautions of bathing and changing his clothes before returning to society.

Unaware of this concern, the animal back in the wilderness could survive on the roughest browsing, and might have some further life in a terrain where wild goats and many other animals were at home. The Israelites were only concerned that it should not return to them with all their wickedness. It was said to be 'For Azazel' – perhaps the name of a desert spirit symbolizing utter remoteness.

At this annual ceremony it was *all* sins and guilt that were dealt with, not just unwitting errors. It was thus felt to be an especially gracious appointment of God to make possible a new start, without which the relation of God and people would be ruined by the accumulation of sins.

And the chief means used for this tremendous enactment of forgiveness and renewal were the lives of the calf and the two goats. No more perfect expression of innocence was known.

The sacrifice of the royal Servant

Earlier in this chapter we considered the vision of salvation in Isaiah 40. That was the begining of a remarkable series of prophecies, and if we follow it through to chapters 52–53, we find that the vision of God's perfect kingdom is not complete without the suffering and victory of his 'Servant'.

From Isaiah 52.13 the voice of God testifies that this his Servant will be triumphant, supreme, anointed to sovereignty (Hebrew *mashachti*) over all mankind, cleansing the nations. But from 53.1 the circle of prophets chant of a great mystery and its unfolding. They tell of the Servant as a king unrecognized, a figure without the appearance of royal beauty. Rather he was like a tormented, diseased person whom all would avoid, considering him punished by God. Then the prophets give the divinely revealed explanation:

> The ailments he bore were ours!
>   Ours were the sufferings he carried!
> There we were, thinking him plagued
>   and smitten by God and punished.
> But it was for our sins he was pierced,
>   and for our misdeeds he was broken.
> On him fell the chastisement for our healing,
>   and through his wounds have we become whole.

This explanation is itself mysterious. But as it is repeated and filled out, there are illuminating references to animals. This royal Servant appears as both shepherd of the people and himself lamb of God. As shepherd he had to suffer for an erring flock:

We had all strayed like a flock,
   we had each gone our own way,
and the Lord brought down on him
   the guilt of all of us.

As lamb of God he was patient, quiet and unresisting:

He was driven, he was afflicted,
   but he did not open his mouth.
Like a lamb to the slaughter was he led,
   and like a ewe silent before her shearers
   he did not open his mouth.

Deprived of the power and rule and respect due to him, the royal Servant was cut off from the land of the living. No harm had he done, but for the people's sins he was smitten. In accordance with God's will, his soul had made an *asham* – a sacrificial offering that made restitution. Against the disobedience, violence and defilements of mankind, the willingness, gentleness and innocence of this chosen Servant would weigh and outweigh. As the blood of innocent lambs had turned away the destroying angels of the Exodus, and as the gentle goats on the day of atonement had carried away a year's load of a people's sins, so the sacrificial life of God's chief Servant would save and set right multitudes of sinners.

And death is not the end of the sacrificed one (so 53.10b–12). For such a life made over to God there is a future, fertile and satisfying, triumphant in the eternal kingdom of God. Such is the divine reward for so truly bearing away the sin of multitudes and interposing for sinners.

Jesus lamb and shepherd

The suffering Servant in Isaiah is not clearly labelled. No name, no time, no place, no circumstance is given. But here

is a work of meekness and majesty without which the kingdom of God is not to be fulfilled.

In a way the Servant is like a divinely inspired idea, which could be embodied by many a good person. But it is a very special idea; in the end we see that it is the Logos, the Word in the sense of John 1.1, the expression of God's heart from the beginning. All who suffer for others manifest this mind of God, this Word, to a degree. They will be owned by Jesus, who is this Word in person, and who fulfilled the Isaiah vision.

One of the most deeply meditated interpretations of Jesus as Saviour is indeed that of St John's Gospel. In chapter 1 John the Baptist sees Jesus and exclaims, 'Behold the lamb of God, who bears away the sin of the world.' In chapter 10 Jesus teaches, 'I am the good shepherd; the good shepherd lays down his life for the sheep . . . I know my own and my own know me, and I lay down my life for the sheep.'

In considering Psalm 23 we saw a figure with the roles of both lamb and shepherd. And now we have seen how for this Gospel Jesus also has the double role. He is the innocent one who, like the atoning lamb and goat, made expiation for sinners, and he is the shepherd who dies for his flock.

Alongside St John's interpretation we can put that of the Letter to the Hebrews. This also offers deep reflection on the sacrificial death of Jesus. The writer sees all the meaning of the temple sacrifices perfectly realized in Jesus. Where the old high priests and their maze of repeated sacrifices fell short, Jesus has once for all made peace with his life offered up. Only he is worthy to enter that most holy Presence, but through him we can enter the new relation with God and find peace.

And so we come to glimpse again that great circle of sacrifice which encompasses the world's meaning. Innocent animals once took the place of man, and in their place has come the Son of Man. Jesus offered the perfect and eternal sacrifice, sending rays of salvation to the beginning and to the end of all things. But the patient animals in their simplicity served to prepare his way, and they live eternally in his love.

In the Chancellor's chariot

Of the many vivid stories in the Acts of the Apostles, that of the Ethiopian takes some beating (Acts 8.26–40). The apostle Philip was prompted by an angel to go out on the desert road to Gaza. There he saw a great Ethiopian minister riding in his chariot – he was returning from a pilgrimage to Jerusalem and was engaged in reading chapter 53 of Isaiah. Philip ran up beside him and enquired how he progressed, only to be invited into the chariot to lead the Bible study. The great man, devout and humble, wanted to know about whom the prophet had said, 'He was led as a sheep to the slaughter, and as a lamb before his shearer is dumb, so he opened not his mouth.' (The slightly different wording was quoted from the Greek translation.)

Beginning with this passage, Philip told him the good news of Jesus. The Ethiopian asked to be baptized and stopped the chariot near water. As they came out of the water, the Spirit mysteriously took Philip away to another mission. The new convert resumed his long journey to Africa with a glad heart. What he did on reaching home is not recorded, but it is a fact of history that the Ethiopians were among the first nations to give their allegiance to Christ and to have the scriptures in their own language.

The story shows again how the early Christians found Christ in the mysterious Servant, and how the image of the innocent animal could be the starting point for unfolding the gospel. The Letter of Peter is another example (I Peter 1.18-20). Not by money (he writes) are we ransomed from the bondage of sin, but by the precious blood of Christ, like that of a beautiful lamb.

She would not have wanted to change her name

One Christmas eve we went to the Farm Animal Sanctuary for carols in the barn. Animals lay quietly in their stalls round the edges. A few sheep and goats wandered among the people, nuzzling them affectionately. A pigeon fluttered across the rafters. A young man with a guitar led the carols, and he was not ruffled when a goat demolished his makeshift music stand of straw bales. Between the carols, in the peace of that shadowy, straw-strewn barn, he told stories about these rescued animals, such as that of the lamb that came to the help of its blind friend. It was easy for him to make connections with Jesus.

We could not but feel that, on this holy night, a blessing came to us through these animals. It was as though the Babe was in this very straw, and a song in the dark skies over Tardebigge. From closeness to these quiet creatures, a soul might well become sensitive to the meaning of Christ's sacrifice and ready to receive his gift of salvation.

On the desert road to Gaza, the pilgrim from distant Africa pondered on the lamb that was slain. His heart was open to Jesus, and he found new life. And there are many others who have travelled through spiritual deserts and have been helped by a patient animal. Moved by the quiet nobility of a suffering creature, they have begun to be cleansed by compassion and love. Whether or not they know it, the suffering Servant, lamb of God, has there embraced them.

Where only a lamb can go

If ever there was a kitten that should have been called Pickle, it was Talitha Eaton. For wherever there was a place unsuitable for kittens, there she was. And whenever there was a time for kittens to hold back, she was to the fore. Her grey and white form, with long neck, small head, big ears, patched face and bright eyes, was everywhere you meant to keep her out from. Mind you, she would not have wanted to change her name. It was spoken by Jesus, and it meant in Aramaic 'little girl' or 'little lamb'.

Having been undernourished in her first three weeks of life, Talitha was determined it would not happen again, and was ever on the watch for a little something. Still today, at the great age of five, she always jumps on my shoulder when I prepare her dish, and wraps herself round the back of my neck, with her head hanging forward to see all is done well and quickly.

One day, feeling her soft fur round my neck, it seemed to me that here at least was one that would speak up for me at the Grand Assize. Sophisticated friends for their own reasons might hold back, but Talitha would just go straight up to the dreadful throne, her tail high, her paws firm on the ground, her eyes earnest, and she would tell her story.

The idea grew, and I thought of some who had been especially kind to earth's little ones. I imagined them tried before the throne one by one, and how, when others held back, the little ones could go fearlessly into the burning Presence, where the mightiest angels could not go; and there they witnessed to kindness that outweighed many faults. These were the beloved children of the house, and mighty was their witness to the heart of the Father who loved them.

Whatever the merits of my imaginings, it is a fact that in the tremendous conclusion of the Bible, the Book of Revelation, the Saviour who alone can go right up to the terrible throne has the appearance and name of a lamb. And as the vision unfolds, it becomes clear that in the supremely gentle, vulnerable one is the supreme power. In the end the lamb who is Christ reigns invincible for ever.

The enraptured seer foresees the terrors and jubilations at the end of this world. A door has opened in heaven (Rev. 4), revealing an amazing scene. On the four sides about the throne of God four heavenly creatures wait and watch, one like a lion, one like an ox, one like a man, and one like an eagle. These lead the worship of God, singing responsively:

Holy, holy, holy,
    is the Lord God Almighty,
who was, and is,
    and is to come.

Outside these creatures is a ring of twenty-four thrones for the elders of the kingdom, and from here the praise swells:

Worthy are you, our Lord and our God,
    to receive the glory, honour and power,
for you created all things,
    and because of your will they came to be
        and were created.

In the hand of God is a scroll sealed with seven seals, and the seer weeps as it seems that none is worthy to open the scroll and launch the drama of the Last Things. But then, inside the ring of thrones, and inside the square of the four Guardians, and so closest of all to the dread throne of God with its lightnings and thunders and flames, appears a lamb.

This lamb seems to have been slaughtered, and yet is standing. This means that his sacrificial death is his eternal glory, which remains with him even in his heavenly life. Without fear, without danger, he is able to approach and receive the scroll from the hand of the Almighty. The heavenly worshippers include him in their praises:

You are worthy to take the scroll
    and to open its seals,
for you were slain, and by your blood
    you have ransomed for God
from every tribe and tongue
    and people and nation.

Worthy is the lamb that was slain
    to receive power and riches
and wisdom and might
    and honour and glory and blessing.

To him that sits upon the throne
    and to the lamb
be blessing and honour and glory and dominion
    for ever and ever, Amen.

The lamb terrible and gentle

And so the lamb breaks open the seals one by one, and with each one terrible episodes of doom ensue. When he opens the sixth seal (6.12), there comes a great earthquake. The sun turns black, and the moon red as blood. The sky throws down its stars as a tree sheds fruit in a gale, and then the sky itself is rolled up like a scroll. Mountains and islands rock from their places. The great and wealthy lead the flight for cover, crying out to be saved from the wrath of the lamb.

But through all this terror, innumerable multitudes are saved and gathered to give glory to God and to the lamb (7.9–10). What is their secret? The seer is told that these have been saved and purified by the lamb's sacrifice; they have 'washed their robes and made them white in the blood of the lamb'. And now the lamb will be their shepherd:

They shall hunger no more,
    nor thirst any more,
neither shall the sun strike upon them,
    nor any heat,
for the lamb in the midst of the throne
    shall be their shepherd,
and shall guide them to springs of living water,
    and God shall wipe all tears from their eyes.

Light and life from the lamb

As this vision of the Last Things continues, yet more titles and glory are seen to belong to the lamb. As Lord of Lords and King of Kings he conquers evil forces (17.14). The marriage of the lamb is announced; his bride is the new Jerusalem (21.9–10), and blessed are those invited to the marriage supper of the lamb (19.7–9). It is all in expression of the coming of the kingdom of good which replaces the present age. Sun and moon are no longer needed, for all is lit by the glory of God and of the lamb. The lamb reigns with God on his throne, from which flows the river of the water of life, nourishing the trees that bring healing to the nations.

The seer's vision is indeed tremendous, overwhelming in its abundance of symbols. It was born in the intensity of a time of persecution, when Roman power set itself cruelly to eliminate the early Christians.

But one thing has been clear in our survey – that the main image of Christ in this work of rich imagery is that of the lamb. From this animal of innocence, harmlessness, vulnerability and sacrifice has come a key of understanding to open ultimate mysteries.

We do well to look with wonder at such creatures. If our heart is open, humble and kind, they will tell us secrets of God's new world, when one like a lamb will become King of Kings.

And those who cruelly use such little ones now should beware. Where will you find shelter in the day of the wrath of the lamb?

6

Animal Praise

Baboons in the congregation

In our last-but-one chapter, an ancient poet showed us the scene at sunrise in the hot Nile valley over three thousand years ago. It was that happy moment when the rays of the early sun shone into the green waters, the fish darted before the face of God, and the birds glided with wings outstretched in praise. The artists of ancient Egypt add to the detail. One portrayed the baboons praising the Creator with their early morning chatter.

We touch here on something very deep, something which is expressed also in the Bible: the universe of praise.

On this matter worshippers of today can still learn from the psalms. It is not so much that our congregations often seem to be of one class and culture, our buildings dull and confining, and not an animal in sight. It is rather that our ideas are confined, our eyes closed to a great reality.

In the psalms the congregation is altogether of a more exciting nature. In many of the praising psalms a singer calls on fellow-worshippers to acclaim and rejoice in God, and it is worth noting who these fellow-worshippers are. In the shortest psalm, for example, they are 'all nations, all peoples' (Ps. 117). In Psalm 29 they are beings in heaven, the angels. In Psalm 96 they are 'the heavens, the earth, the sea and all that lives in it . . . the countryside and all that is in it . . . all the trees of the forest'. All these, according to the psalm, form a host of worshippers united in dancing and singing before the face of the Lord who has shown his Presence in their midst.

Psalm 98 is similar, but the rejoicing is described in some detail. There is responsive singing with accompaniment of plucked strings, trumpets and horns. The sea leads the universal praise with a thunderous roar, the torrents clap their hands, the mountains sing and echo.

But Psalm 148 lists the fellow-worshippers in more detail. First are addressed the heavenly beings who speed on God's errands. Then come sun and moon and stars of light. Then the highest skies and the blue ocean of heaven. Next come sea-monsters and deeps. Then fire, hail, snow, frost and storm-wind. The call to sing is further given to mountains, fruit trees and cedars, along with all animals, wild and domestic, all things creeping and all things flying. And at last the call moves round to the various sorts of humans – the rulers and the ruled, old and young, all nations, and the Israelites.

The music of animals

The whole thrilling experience of universal praise is encapsulated in the concluding psalm, 150. Here the call to praise is addressed first to the beings of heavens and skies, then to the worshippers in the temple with their numerous instruments and dances, and lastly to 'all breath' – everything living. The musical instruments are mentioned in detail, and the context suggests how their contribution has a representative character. It appears that the players and the dancers in the open court of the temple express the voice and movement of all creatures.

In modern times there has been a movement towards the

use of 'period instruments'. The earlier forms of woodwind, strings etc. are preferred for early music. Not only is there a certain logic in using instruments for which the composer actually wrote. The sounds themselves have a peculiar charm, more intimate and more natural. In the same way the currently popular pan-pipes have a special appeal, as they seem to catch the sound of wind on reed beds and birds of the mountains.

So in the open-air court of the temple, the blowing of the ram's horn, the sweeping and plucking of harps and lyres, the tapping of the skin frame-drums, the blowing of pipes (whether flutes, oboes or clarinets), the tinkling and shivering of the various kinds of cymbals, the whisper of shakers, the chatter of clackers – all related to sounds of nature, just as the circling dances related to the movement of the living world. The temple itself was thought of as a focal point in the universe, a concentration of vast meaning in a small place. And so also the dancers and musicians praising the Lord were expressing the dance and song of all the living things around God.

We are familiar with the teaching of Jesus that we should be in good relation with our fellows before we come close to God in his temple. If our fellow has a grievance against us, we should put down our offering and go off to make good the wrong, and only then return to make our offering (Matt. 5.23–24). But when God opens our eyes to see the vast circle of the congregation, to know the universal fellowship of praise that includes all living creatures of sea, air and land, then we have much wrong to put right before we can properly enter God's presence. We must search our hearts and repent of all the uncaring, vandalizing, unkind sides to our ways with God's living world. As Job teaches us, even the furrows of our soil should not have cause to weep and complain against us, if we are to be at peace with God (Job 31.38–40).

A key to the universes

A few years ago I heard a soulful performance of the Sea Symphony of Vaughan Williams in the little Cornish town of Saint Austell, where seagulls glide and call. For lack of a concert hall, the performance was in the Methodist church. We were sitting in the gallery, as also was the choir, while conductor, orchestra and soloists were below. The work opens with impressions of boisterous seas, and so heartily did the Cornish brass and drums render their parts, that plaster began to rain down on us from the ceiling. In spite of our natural anxieties, the music, with the words of Walt Whitman, soon claimed all our attention.

From the image of the great ocean and its brave voyagers, thought develops of the voyage into the vast spiritual world. The boisterous music dies away. A solemn quietness finds the poet alone on the beach at night. The sea sways to and fro, an old mother singing her husky song, and the stars shine above. Then the poet thinks 'a thought of the clef of the universes and of the future'. It is the thought of that which interlocks, holds and encloses all identities, all that has ever existed and will ever exist, all times and spaces, all lives and deaths.

That which so spans and holds is called by the poet 'a vast similitude' − whatever idea we have of it could be but a likeness, a parable of it. But to be aware of this supreme reality, which connects and holds all identities in eternal meaning, is to know 'the clef of the universes and of the future'.

A 'clef' is a key, and in music the various clefs are keys to the way to read all the following notes. In the Bible 'the clef of the universes' might be found in the expression 'Halleluia' (meaning 'Praise the Lord'). For the essential is not that there is a God and a world made by him alone, but that the world exists by relation to him, the relation which from the human side is called 'praise'. The whole and healthy universe is a myriad of identities turned to the centre in praise. Praise acknowledges the divine Creator, recognizes in him the eternal source of being, gazes on him in humility, love and joy. In so turning to God the creatures have fullness of life, and are connected with each other as a vast living body.

But are we speaking of the world we know? Is not this universe of praise rather an ideal, a vision of what should be? Yes it is. But it is also a meaning which is shining into the present imperfect world, and calling to us to live by its light.

In the psalms of ecstatic praise (such as 8, 24, 47, 93, 96–99, 148, 150) there is celebration of the Creator who has 'become king' and 'entered' in glory. The world is made new, and all is gladness and peace. Commentators are hard put to it to explain the experience celebrated in these psalms. It is too perfect to be the present world, but it is too present to be the future world!

So we come back to our 'clef of the universes and of the future'. Such psalms came from an exalted moment in the great festivals, when the Halleluia-key opened up the vision of universal praise. In that moment the universe was praising God and living through that praise. And the praise itself was the reflecting back of the beauty and light and power of life which had shone first from God to each one of his creatures. The vision of a perfect world was even at that moment irradiating the present world, uncovering a meaning that was hidden in it, enabling the worshippers to have a part in it.

In the Battersea Dogs' Home there was a great cacophony. Dogs with high voices, dogs with low voices, yelpers, growlers, all added to the din. It was not the sound of animal praise. It was the sound of vexation and nerves disturbed. For these were dogs that had suffered from human unkindness. They had yet to find peace in this temporary shelter of goodwill.

And then a strange, unearthly sound was heard. It was the singing of hump-back whales, played from a recording. The dogs behind their wires fell silent. They looked quizzical, then began to settle on their beds. They yawned and relaxed, and soon began to doze.

Could it be that the song of the whales had brought an echo of the universal praise, opening that world of torn relations to the healing light of the Creator? The recording had caught the music of the mighty creatures enjoying happy freedom in the element for which they were made. They were responding to the gift of life, and their voices were able to call other creatures into that interchange of peace.

Holding on to praise and the circle of love

According to the Greek version of the Book of Daniel, a great Halleluia was sung by the three faithful young men who were thrown into the fiery furnace. Their persecutors were amazed to see them unharmed, and comforted by a fourth figure beside them in the flames, one like a son of man. The story can be a parable to us. In the worst afflictions of this world we must still sing the Halleluia, and see through to the joyful universe that dances and sings in love to the Creator. That world beyond will take reality around us as we sing and go forth with our song.

The song which the three sang in the furnace was one of the greatest songs of universal praise. Beyond the jealousy, greed and cruelty of the human oppressors, they reached out to the wonderful creatures of earth and sea and skies, and united in a harmony of love and praise.

After blessing God in his glory, the song continues with calls to all elements and creatures to join the praise:

O all ye Works of the Lord, bless ye the Lord,
   praise him and magnify him for ever.
O ye Angels of the Lord, bless ye the Lord,
   praise him and magnify him for ever.
O ye Waters that be above the firmament,
   bless ye the Lord,
     praise him and magnify him for ever.
O all ye Powers of the Lord, bless ye the Lord,
   praise him and magnify him for ever.
O all ye Powers of the Lord bless ye the Lord,
   praise him and magnify him for ever.
O ye Sun and Moon, bless ye the Lord,
   praise him and magnify him for ever.
O ye Stars of heaven, bless ye the Lord,
   praise him and magnify him for ever.
O ye Showers and Dew, bless ye the Lord,
   praise him and magnify him for ever.
O ye Winds of God, bless ye the Lord,
   praise him and magnify him for ever.
O ye Fire and Heat, bless ye the Lord,
   praise him and magnify him for ever.
O ye Winter and Summer, bless ye the Lord,
   praise him and magnify him for ever.
O ye Dews and Frosts, bless ye the Lord,
   praise him and magnify him for ever.
O ye Ice and Snow, bless ye the Lord,
   praise him and magnify him for ever.
O ye Nights and Days, bless ye the Lord,
   praise him and magnify him for ever.
O ye Light and Darkness, bless ye the Lord,
   praise him and magnify him for ever.
O ye Lightnings and Clouds, bless ye the Lord,
   praise him and magnify him for ever.
O let the Earth bless the Lord,
   yea, let it praise him and magnify him for ever.

O ye Mountains and Hills, bless ye the Lord,
    praise him and magnify him for ever.
O all ye Green Things upon the earth, bless ye the Lord,
    praise him and magnify him for ever.
O ye Wells, bless ye the Lord,
    praise him and magnify him for ever.
O ye Seas and Floods, magnify the Lord,
    praise him and magnify him for ever.
O ye Whales and all that move in the waters,
    bless ye the Lord,
    praise him and magnify him for ever.
O all ye Beasts and Cattle, bless ye the Lord,
    praise him and magnify him for ever.
O ye Children of Men, bless ye the Lord,
    praise him and magnify him for ever . . .
O ye Spirits and Souls of the righteous, bless ye the Lord,
    praise him and magnify him for ever . . .
O ye holy and humble Men of heart, bless ye the Lord,
    praise him and magnify him for ever . . .

Beside the River Mersey stood St Mary's church, a neo-Gothic building large enough to be a cathedral. I recall the services of fifty or sixty years ago as rather colourless, and certainly hard work for the faithful choir. Welcome indeed were the sweets passed round under the pew-tops during the lessons (which were sometimes as much as sixty verses each) and sermon (delivered from a grand pulpit). Over the years, the congregation grew smaller in the vast spaces, and the chanting of the old full quotas of psalms and canticles, accompanied by a strongly played organ, was a strenuous task. But there you met unpretentious people, especially good-hearted and loyal.

And often at Sunday matins we sang the song just quoted, the Benedicite (meaning 'Bless ye'). On top of all the other items, it was a lot to sing in that great place, but it came as a refreshment. That was a parish where no one had a garden, and acres of poisoned industrial waste land, deserted since the great Depression, stretched all around. But in the Benedicite we were joined with angels and stars, with waters and whales, with winds and frosts and fire, with all spirits and souls of all ages, in the praise of the Creator, and we received a blessing beyond all we knew at the time.

In more recent years, the River Mersey has grown cleaner and the waste lands have been reclaimed, so that cattle can graze there. May the song of the Three Holy Children, the Benedicite, ever echo there! With such a song we turn the key of release from our prison of human self-preoccupation. We open a vista to the world which always was, and is yet to be, the world where all beings, all identities, share in the love and praise of God, and are at peace with each other.

7

Recollecting our Journey

Fresh air

They came from the concrete jungle, where the only roar was the never-ending roar of traffic. They were one of the parties of children brought from the inner city for a few hours with the animals around Tardebigge. Janet Taylor relates how the cheery crowd, wanting to pick up everything that moved, was suddenly reduced to an awed silence as Lucy the massive pig lumbered up to greet them. The children were undecided whether to run for their lives or remain rooted to the spot. But Lucy soon won them over and they patted her with delight. They hugged every animal that could be hugged, and ran from paddock to paddock until they were quite worn out.

Before they left, Janet asked one pale-faced little boy what he had enjoyed most. He looked round slowly. All about him were hens and dogs, and somone was still clutching a lamb. The animals had all done their part for the children. The sheep had nuzzled them. The goats had staged a mock battle. The ponies had licked them. The boy thought about it all, then he sniffed and answered, 'I liked the hoxygen best, Miss.'

The child had spoken wisely. He had picked on something fundamental to the whole. In the whole system of life, air is of vital importance, and it is something which the selfish and callous ways of our society are grievously spoiling around his home. That day he had had a total experience. The people were kind, the children and animals had met each other in love, and for all of them the air was good. Our journey through the Bible texts has concentrated on animals, but again and again we have been prompted to see the life of the earth as one living community, with wind and waters, mountains and trees, animals and peoples belonging together in the hand of the Creator.

First recollections of our way

After a long journey it is good to be still awhile and reflect on the way we have come. We don't recall all the details, but moments of special significance come back to us and help us to collect ourselves and orient our resolve for the days ahead. So now, let us reflect on our pilgrimage through the animal paths of the Bible – truly a Saints' Way.

First we encountered some fundamentals. The Creation stories of Genesis were basic. These were like a kind of poem which took up great values and presented them as part of the very fabric of life. They showed animals as wonderful creatures of God, beloved by him, and entrusted by him into the care of humanity. We were to be God's faithful stewards in the living world, strong, but answerable to him.

In seeing all as originally vegetarian, the poetic stories reflected the enduring intuition that the Creator's purpose was to make a society of love before his face, with all animals and people living together in peace and trust. The scriptures saw this as an ideal that had been broken, but that would be restored again.

Yet looking down the centuries before and after Christ, we saw many examples of this ideal already shining effectively into the present world. There were many wonderful moments of trust between the species, times of holy companionship, with no harming. And even when the era of killing prevailed, the ancient people had laws and restrictions which upheld reverence for living things. Responsibility before the Creator opposed the instincts of greed and cruelty.

Often on our pilgrimage through the texts we found that the Bible mentioned characteristics of animals as a reproach to the self-importance and hypocrisies of humans. We met a donkey that was alive to the awesome presence of God, when the holy men and princes saw nothing. It was she who made possible the fulfilment of the prophet's mission, when the creative words about David and the Messiah were flung out on the air from the mountain tops.

Responsive to the Creator's will, animals served in many other great moments. The mysterious events by which the Lord installed his first Anointed, his royal Servant, began with donkeys that followed God's prompting. And a prophet's vision of the Messiah riding into Jerusalem was symbolically fulfilled by Jesus, with a donkey playing an important part, expressing the divine will for the world's salvation by way of humility and gentleness.

We were intrigued to see the friendship of birds and people represented in great biblical scenes. For Noah there were the birds skilled in navigation, and for Elijah the birds that would befriend a good and lonely person. The birds had gifts of flight, eye-sight and intelligence which they could bring to the aid of our earth-bound species. And their wonderful way of life, their beauty, and their wisdom were found to be full of lessons for human beings. Birds truly were messengers from the heavens.

Without the devastating weapons and swift transport of modern man, the ancients might have had more excuse for fearing and destroying the great predators such as lions and leopards. But the Bible saw all these formidable animals in a spiritual perspective. They came beautiful from God's hand, wise from his instruction. They lived under his guidance and by his provision. They called to him in need, and responded to his promptings to serve him in judgment and mercy.

Memories of animal wisdom

As we took our way through the paths of proverbs, we found that the ancient sages spoke much of animals and plants. Even in small creatures, such as ants, locusts, rock-hyraxes and geckos, the sages found much to contemplate. The way to wisdom was to look at these animals with love, humility, and a heart open to receive. And here, still more, was a way to find God their Creator. To the watching, wondering, tender heart God could disclose himself and convert us to a life of love.

Also on our way we met domestic animals that vitally served human need with patience and gentleness. Such were the camels that carried rider or burden through otherwise impossible hardships. The test for the future mother of Israel, Rebekah, was whether she would show kindness to the camels, and so demonstrate that she was in tune with God's own kindness.

We found that the importance of animals in the hearts and imagination of the biblical people was shown in some surprising ways. There was the naming of children after animals. There were the animal forms which loomed up in the mist of poetry of Creation, with thoughts of chaos changed into living order. There were also the animal shapes that visionaries saw in the presence of God, beings that were his attendants and helpers, able to tread the dreadful holy ground. The Book of Job told us with glittering eloquence of the shapes of chaos, mighty animal forms which lived happily before God's face. Here was chaos transformed into beauty, but a beauty that would bring beholders to their knees in unspeakable adoration of the Creator.

We came upon tapestries of animals, scenes of many and varied figures, with many colours and delicate beauties. The tapestries were inspired by the infinitely great and wondrous pattern of the living world, the one web of universal life made up of numerous kinds. In ancient Egypt and later in the psalms, the pattern was deeply seen – a world enfolded in the care of God – and prayer was made against the wickedness that would spoil the world.

How we came to the lamb of God

Passing now through the rocky wilderness that borders and penetrates the Holy Land, we followed the shepherds' way. Deep were the thoughts aroused by the harmless lamb and goat. From these creatures had arisen a mighty icon of sacrifice, a powerful symbol of purity that by God's will would be set in opposition to the sin of the world. This symbol was the rallying point for the saving powers of divine forgiveness and human repentance, which together would break the grip of evil.

So Jesus appeared as the lamb, the lamb slain but standing, the lamb that bears away the sin of the world, the lamb slain from the foundation of the world. In the symbol of the lamb and goat, his work was brought to our hearts. In the symbols of the wrath of the lamb and the lamb sharing the Father's throne, there went out a word dreadful to the loveless, the callous – the word that Love is the conqueror and the sovereign to all eternity.

What the animal voices meant

The last stage of our pilgrimage brought us into the great circle of creatures that praise the Lord. We were amazed to reflect how congregations that had sung the psalms, the Benedicite, the hymn of blessed Saint Francis, and similar songs, had for centuries failed to take the words seriously and see the universal circle of creatures singing all around them. On their lips were lines about the praising sun and stars, winds, waves, whales and trees, all animals and birds. But they were more likely to regard it all as some poetic fancy than as a vitally important reality. And a sermon to correct them might not have been given for hundreds of years.

So we burned to cry out that now it was high time for the self-centred, self-importrant generations of humans to awake to reality and enter the world of true worship and praise. For in the kingdom of God all living things dance and sing in their own manner to the glory of God. Through the bond of each with the Ever-Creator all living things relate to each other in love and respect. Only in the spirit of reconciliation to every fellow-member of the congregation of the universes could we humans offer praise pleasing to God.

The bard of Orkney

Our experience of animal praise connected with our thoughts on the Creation stories. It brings to mind the world of the Dreaming – a glorious world before time was, and after time shall end, and yet hovering about us now, thinly screened from us, and now and then shining into our broken world. Even now, if we sing the songs of universal praise, willing to hear through love the halleluias of all things that have life, we begin to have a part in that true world.

A striking poet who came from Orkney, Edwin Muir, told in his poem 'The Transfiguration' of an experience when that better world appeared to him. All was in its place:

> The painted animals
> Assembled there in gentle congregations,
> Or sought apart their leafy oratories,
> Or walked in peace, the wild and tame together.

People stepped free from their dungeons, from the shackles of their crimes, from entanglements of their own devices, from labyrinths of loneliness. Edwin was seeing the love and glory of the eternal world, usually invisible to our soiled eyes, but working ever and everywhere. Not as a thin and fleeting hope did that world appear, but as the truly existing, the truly enduring. It seemed that if the showing of it had lasted but another moment, it might have held for ever.

Edwin concluded his poem with thought of the future hope. Not for mankind alone would Christ bring in that true world of gentleness and trust:

> for all things,
> Beasts of the field, and woods, and rocks, and seas,
> And all mankind from end to end of the earth
> Will call him with one voice.

The tormented wood of the crucifixion would become a tree in a green corner of Eden, and Judas would take his long journey to childhood innocence, and his betrayal be quite undone, never more to be done.

The experience described in that poem should not be regarded as something given only to rare souls, the born poets. Still less should it be treated as something to be boxed away in a neat book on its proper shelf, aside from practical living. It is but another expression of what the biblical people commonly knew in their pilgrimages and festivals, their great moments of worship. For there the true world shone through. The Lord reigned. The sin of our passing world was countered and cleansed by sacrifice, and penitence passed into praise. Song and dance celebrated the Creator who makes all things new and reigns eternally as the caring Lord of every living thing.

And what they beheld in the great showings of worship sent a light through ordinary days. In their homes, their fields, their industries, their markets, they could make spaces for the kingdom of God, windows for the light of the compassionate world where all the species were united around the glory of the Creator.

Messages brought from our travels

From our journey through the Bible's words on animals we bring two special messages. For those who relate easily to God but not much to compassion for animals, the message is to beware of complicity in a great human crime, centuries old, and virulent still. If you would be servants of the living God you must answer to him for your care of all that lives, the care he has entrusted to you.

For those who relate easily to compassion for animals but not much to God, the One that is not ourselves, the message is to beware of trust in one's own resource, strength and virtue. The drama of good and evil, kindness and cruelty, is universal, of cosmic proportions. So let your kindness, your zeal of love, flow from a heart humble before the Lord. Your work will not of itself attain lasting success. No campaigns, no laws will see off human wickedness. But do all you can for the sake of him who showed himself to us as a lamb slain from the foundation of the world. Do all you can with his help and blessing and guidance, and your love will be taken up into his eternal working, and multiplied beyond all your imagining.

You will know, yes you *will* know, the time when the thin wall will be broken through, the true world appear, and the creatures you have loved will come around you in their multitudes, affectionate, and content for ever.

Some words of Anna and Jesus

Ivor has lent me a very large book of animals. Actually, it was a present he gave Carol, his wife, but she is a good soul and will not mind. It is called *The Ark* and is the work of the Dutch artist, Rien Poortvliet. Loosely following the theme of the Flood story, he has filled the large pages with his gentle paintings of animals, scattering comments here and there. His painting of the Ark's timbers and the wild waters and skies is as vivid as his presentation of the great variety of animals.

On one page he has put several paintings of a young hare, and he tells the story of a six-year old Austrian girl, Anna. She nursed the ophaned hare, feeding it with a bottle, but alas, it did not survive. For its epitaph she wrote: 'Oh my darling pet, I loved you, and I love you still, in the name of the Father, and of the Son, and of the Holy Spirit.'

In this simple statement of Anna's there is great depth. Such love endures. The loved one, dead from this world, yet lives and can be addressed. And the whole truth of the love and eternity is enfolded in the revelation of the Creator. Under the light of God the glorious truth is seen, that love abides for ever.

But let our last thought be of a saying of Jesus. In his last days in Jerusalem he knew that the city would treat him no better than it treated great prophets of old. 'Oh Jerusalem, Jerusalem,' he lamented, 'killing the prophets and stoning those sent to you! How often I would have gathered your children together as a hen gathers her chicks under her wings, but you would not have it so!' (Matt. 23.37; Luke 13.34).

On the one hand, the picture of a human community, in many ways privileged, but falling murderously on the inconvenient messengers of God. On the other hand, the image of a hen caring for her chicks, gathering them to the safe shelter of her wings – an image which discloses the divine love. Jesus evidently had seen and deeply known the beautiful scene of hen and chicks.

Such was the Saviour who had prepared for his work by

dwelling in the wilderness with the wild animals (Mark 1.13). The ancient time had come again, and the Tempter came with his wiles. But Jesus stood firm, and the animals surrounded him without harm. The angels had no task now to bar the way to the kingdom of peace, but comforted and served the faithful Lord of the Creatures.

In the spirit of Jesus, we ask for the gift of a caring, compassionate heart as we look at the living world, with all its necessary kinds. Already, without delay, if we wish, we can have part in the true world, the universe of love.

Notes

In chapter 1, for a selection of the writings of the hermit Isaac see *Heart of Compassion, Daily Readings with St Isaac of Syria*, edited by A.M. Allchin (Darton, Longman & Todd 1989).

In chapter 3, details of the ancient use of birds in navigation can be found in the academic study of Othmar Keel, *Vögel als Boten* (Universitätsverlag, Freiburg 1979). Keel also gives the story of Meginrat and the ravens, and argues for the ceremonial release of doves in Israelite festivals.

In chapter 4, the birth of the pony on the Welsh moors was witnessed by Pamela Rowlands Smith and described by her in a letter published in the *Daily Mail* of 13 May 1994.

In chapter 5, for 'The sacrifice of the royal Servant' you may like to compare the longer exposition in my *Interpreted By Love* (Bible Reading Fellowship 1994) pp. 121–135, including a note on 'anointed' in Isa. 52.14 on p. 158.

In chapter 7, the quotation from Edwin Muir's 'The Transfiguration' is taken from his *Collected Poems 1921–1951* (Faber & Faber 1952, pp. 173–75) and used by permission. Rien Poortvliet's *The Ark* (1986) is published by Lion Publishing.

Index of Biblical References